GW00669614

OLD LIVERPOOL FC IN COLOUR

OLD LIVERPOOL FC IN COLOUR

Reach Sport

OLD LIVERPOOL FC IN COLOUR

Hardback edition first published in Great Britain in 2022
www.reachsport.com
@reach_sport
Reach Sport is a part of Reach PLC Ltd, 5 St Paul's Square, Liverpool, L3 9SJ
One Canada Square, Canary Wharf, London, E15 5AP

Hardback ISBN: 9781914197390

Photo colourisation: George Chilvers
Writer and researcher: Mark Platt
Designers: Colin Sumpter, Lee Ashun
Production editor: Roy Gilfoyle
Cover design: Colin Sumpter

Photographic acknowledgements:
Mirrorpix, Liverpool Football Club, Getty Images, Colorsport and private collections.

Printed and bound by Bell & Bain Ltd, Glasgow.

OLD LIVERPOOL FC
IN COLOUR

ONTENTS

'RELIVE THE RISE OF THE REDS LIKE YOU'VE NEVER DONE BEFORE'

The history of Liverpool Football Club is a rich and colourful tapestry, made up by a cast of thousands and spanning 130 years. For the majority of the first century of the club's existence though, it was a story predominantly documented only in black and white.

Old Liverpool FC In Colour redresses that balance by shedding new light on this now seemingly long lost age of monochrome football photography – and, in doing so, breathes renewed vigour into a well-versed narrative.

Through the expert colourisation of a meticulously-curated collection of archive images, the players, personalities, triumphs and travails of a club that rose from humble origins to become the undisputed Kings of Europe are vibrantly brought to life in the modern era.

From the blue and white shirted 'Team of Macs' and inaugural title-winning red men, to the 'Untouchables' of the early 1920s and the post-war 'Crazy Gang'. Kopites with flat caps to mop tops in suits, through the eras of Liddellpool and Shanks, to the stars of the Seventies and heroes of the Eighties. League titles, cup wins and adventures abroad, the influential figures, important games and unforgettable moments.

Until someone invents a way to travel back in time, this is the closest we will ever get to seeing the rise of Liverpool as it would have been viewed by our ancestors, who were lucky enough to experience it first-hand all those years ago.

For this, we have the hugely talented George Chilvers to thank. An undisputed expert in the field of colouring old football photographs, there

BUTLERS

was only ever one candidate to take on the task of this massive project and he's done a remarkable job in diligently working his way through over 130 photographs in less than a year (he explains his process on p180).

While it's said that a picture can paint a thousand words, we also wanted to provide some added context around each image and tell the hidden story behind what you see.

Although the majority of photographs run chronologically, the short stories that accompany each are written in a way that allows the option for readers to either dip in and out of the story at their leisure or simply follow the familiar path from start to finish.

Choosing and sourcing the photographs came first though and, while this was a real labour of love, the actual selection process was far from easy. With access to such vast archives as those belonging to Liverpool Football Club and Mirrorpix, not to mention the likes of Getty, Colorsport and other private collections, to say we were spoilt for choice would be an understatement.

Rather than just opting for a random bunch of pictures, each one was carefully selected so that it fitted into the overall sequence of events, and that collectively they take the reader on a seamless journey from the club's formation in 1892 to its last Football League title in 1990.

The decision to not go beyond the first century is purely down to the fact that almost every picture taken since then will have already been seen in colour by at least some fans.

It was never the intention to just recount every famous player, big victory, cup final or major moment and so you'll find that some lesser-known names or events are often given more prominence than seemingly higher-profile figures and occasions. It's not an oversight, just the nature of the book.

The quality of the actual photograph was another determining factor in the selection process and, similarly, we were mindful of ensuring that there's a mix of styles, i.e. action images, team groups and general portrait/landscape shots.

Where possible we've also opted for pictures that have rarely, or never, been published before, and we'd like to think that there is more than a fair share of these among the final total.

Alongside them are some of the more obvious iconic images that just couldn't be overlooked because of their relevance or importance. If our research is correct though, the majority won't ever have been published in colour before.

'TRAWLING THROUGH OLD PHOTOGRAPHS HAS NEVER BEEN MORE POPULAR. THEY RECONNECT US WITH THE PAST IN A WAY NO OTHER MEDIUM ALLOWS AND BRING PRECIOUS MEMORIES FLOODING BACK. IN THE YEAR WE CELEBRATE OUR 130TH ANNIVERSARY, OLD LIVERPOOL FC IN COLOUR IS A CELEBRATION OF THE CLUB'S FASCINATING HERITAGE'

Of course, in this age of social media, images are being posted and shared far more freely than ever before so it's becoming increasingly difficult to track what is actually out there in the public domain but, in turn, this has led to an increased craving for nostalgia of this kind.

Trawling through old photographs has seemingly never been more popular. They reconnect us with the past in a way no other medium allows and bring precious memories flooding back and generate fresh discussion about that particular subject matter.

Hopefully, this book will serve the exact same purpose and, with every picture having been revitalised in full colour, provide an even more immersive experience.

So, sit back, relax, and allow yourself to be transported back in time, to the scenes that play out through the pages of this book, and relive the rise of the Reds like you've never done before.

In the year we celebrate our 130th anniversary, *Old Liverpool FC In Colour* is a unique celebration of the club's fascinating heritage. Enjoy the journey.

Up The Reds!

Mark Platt, 2022

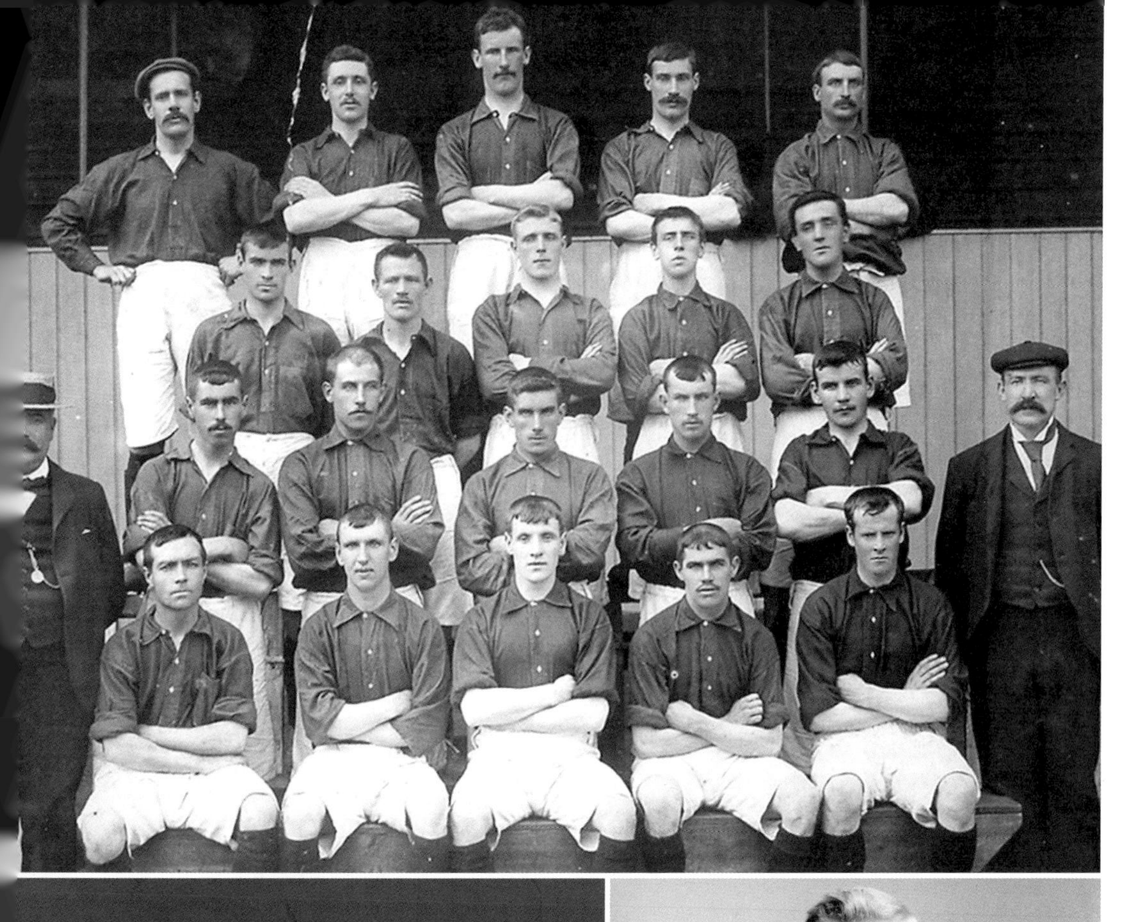

EARLY IMPRESSIONS...1890s

1. THE CREATOR SUPREME

Without John Houlding there would be no Liverpool Football Club as we know it today, and so it is with this man that the story naturally begins.

A self-made businessman and politician, who would later become Lord Mayor of the city, Houlding owned a brewery and a string of pubs, including the now famous Sandon Hotel on Oakfield Road.

His influence on how the professional game in this region developed is unsurpassed. Known locally as 'King John', he was, at first, a key figure in the formative years of Everton Football Club; securing the acquisition of Anfield and overseeing their first league title success.

The explosive boardroom split of 1892, however, shook the club to its core and resulted in the majority of Everton members taking the club across Stanley Park to Goodison Park.

This left Houlding with a dilemma. He had a first-class ground but no team to play in it. Yet, rather than give up on football, he decided to form a new club.

It was to be an inspired move that would change the landscape of football on Merseyside forever.

Liverpool FC was born, and he ploughed his own personal fortune into making it a success, occupying the role of chairman and then president until his death in 1902. During this time, he helped the club make rapid strides and lay the all-important foundations for everything that came afterwards.

Back row (left to right): *Joe McQue, John McCartney, Andrew Hannah, Sydney Ross, Matt McQueen, Duncan McLean, Jim McBride, Alec Dick (trainer).*
Front row: *Tom Wylie, Jock Smith, John Miller, Malcolm McVean, Hugh McQueen.*

2. TEAM OF MACS

In pale blue and white halved shirts that had been inherited from Anfield's previous tenants, this is the first known photograph of a Liverpool team.

It is believed to have been taken outside the original Main Stand, sometime around November or December 1892.

Nine of the players pictured here had featured in the club's inaugural fixture – a 7-1 friendly victory against Rotherham Town on 1 September 1892, with John Miller scoring the historic opening goal.

Two of those that didn't play – the McQueen brothers, Matt and Hugh – were not signed until October 1892 and this side first lined up together in the game away to Fleetwood Rangers on 12 November 1892.

With every player on this photograph born north of the border, it was a team that could have represented Scotland and therefore the 'Team of Macs' was an obvious moniker that was quickly bestowed on them.

Due to an administrative error that denied the fledgling club a place in the Football League, it was in the Lancashire League that these players competed during the 1892/93 season.

Plying their trade in front of modest home crowds that averaged just 2,441 over the course of the campaign, they clicked immediately and pipped Blackpool to the title on goal average.

Even sweeter would have been the result of that season's Liverpool Senior Cup final, which saw Houlding's new club defeat his old club to clinch a memorable double.

3. HONEST JOHN

There can be no doubting John McKenna's status as one of the most important and influential figures in the early history of Liverpool Football Club.

A footballing pioneer who became a close aide of John Houlding during their time together at Everton, McKenna stayed loyal to Houlding and would be a key component in Liverpool's rise.

Ambitious and forward-thinking, the Irishman held a prominent position within the boardroom and was viewed as the public face of the club.

Entrusted with the task of assembling Liverpool's first ever team, he had organised the inspirational recruitment drive north of the border, from which the now famous 'Team of Macs' evolved.

Initially, McKenna shared secretarial and managerial duties with William Barclay but was very much considered to be the more influential partner in this relationship.

McKenna was one of the game's great administrators and, following a season in the Lancashire League, it was he who instigated and oversaw the club's successful assimilation into the Football League.

Although he would later take a back seat regarding team affairs, his presence in and around the club remained huge for years to come, continuing as a director until 1921 and twice taking on the role of chairman.

In addition to the high esteem in which McKenna was held at Liverpool, he was also a much-respected figure throughout football due to his position as president of the Football League from 1917 until his death in 1936.

No. 35668 C.

N.L. 34731.

Certificate of Change of Name

OF THE

Everton Football Club and Athletic Grounds Company, Limited.

I hereby Certify, That the Everton Football Club and Athletic Grounds Company, Limited, having, with the sanction of a **Special Resolution** of the said Company, and with the approval of the BOARD OF TRADE, changed its name, is now called the Liverpool Football Club and Athletic Grounds Company, Limited, and I have entered such new name on the Register accordingly.

Given under my hand at London this Third day of June One Thousand Eight Hundred and Ninety Two.

[signature]

Registrar of Joint Stock Companies.

4. THE UNBEATEN ANFIELDERS

At the back of the Sandon Hotel, which then also doubled up as the unofficial headquarters of Liverpool Football Club, the players and directors pose for a photograph to commemorate their acceptance into the Football League for the 1893/94 season.

The identity of the dog remains unknown, but handlebar moustaches are seemingly all the rage among the players, while bowler hats look to be the headwear of choice for directors.

Chairman John Houlding sits proudly at the centre of the front row, no doubt content in the knowledge that, while it's still early days, his gamble to form Liverpool Football Club is already showing signs of paying off.

Although the shirts are still pale blue and white, another exciting new chapter is set to unfold. Along with Arsenal, they have been admitted to the Second Division and it was to be a victorious campaign.

With a handful of new signings added to the core of the team that had won the Lancashire League, promotion was stylishly clinched at the first attempt.

Jimmy Stott top scored, registering 14 goals in just 17 appearances, while Duncan McLean and Matt McQueen featured in all but one of the games as Liverpool powered through an unbeaten season in the league and without dropping a single point at home – a feat that no Anfield team is yet to emulate.

THE UNBEATEN ANFIELDERS (MAIN PICTURE ON NEXT PAGE)

Back row (left to right): *John Dermott, Benjamin Bailey, Sydney Cooper, Thomas C Howarth, Alexander Nisbet, Harry Cooper, Charles Gibson, Henry Ellis, Lawrence Crosswaite (all directors).*
Middle row: *John McCartney, Matt McQueen, Andrew Hannah (captain), Billy McOwen, Duncan McLean, Douglas Dick, James Henderson, T Whitway (trainer).*
Front row: *Patrick Gordon, Malcolm McVean, Joe McQue, Jim McBride, John McKenna (director), John Houlding (chairman), James Ramsey (director), Harry Bradshaw, Jimmy Stott, Hugh McQueen.*

Caption on page 21

5. WATSON'S RED REVOLUTION

A rare portrait of Tom Watson, the longest-serving manager in Anfield history, pictured here without his trademark bowler hat or straw boater.

During his remarkable 19-year reign, Watson would revolutionise the club and take it on to another level, firmly establishing Liverpool as one of the leading teams in the country.

A native of the north-east, he was recruited by John McKenna from Sunderland, where his 'Team Of All The Talents' had won three First Division titles.

Although still only 37 at the time of his appointment, Watson's reputation as the most successful secretary-manager in the game at this time was more than justified and his capture, in July 1896, was viewed as a real coup for Liverpool.

A reflection of the club's ambitious plans for the future, it also signalled a major shift in policy regarding team management at Anfield.

Managerial and secretarial duties had previously been split between McKenna and Barclay but Watson would combine both roles to great effect.

Renowned as an innovative tactician and a great leader of men, he immediately implemented a new training regime and ordered his players to follow a strict diet.

Together with some astute new signings, the club would now fully emerge from the shadow of elder neighbours Everton and soon be challenging for the top honours.

Highly respected and much-loved, Tom Watson remained as manager until his sudden death in 1915, by which time two league championships had been celebrated, a first appearance in the FA Cup final secured and a legacy left that would reap even more success in later years.

V
1901

6. ALEX THE GREAT

Liverpool's first superstar footballer, Alex Raisbeck, is captured here in the old primrose yellow and rose pink colours of his native Scotland.

Acquired from Hibernian in July 1898, Raisbeck would prove to be one of the best signings ever made by the club. It required a then substantial fee of £350 to bring him to Anfield but it was money more than well spent.

Although only 19 at the time, the future international had forged a reputation as one of the most promising players north of the border and a loan spell at Stoke proved he was also well capable of cutting it in the English First Division.

John McKenna and Tom Watson were already well aware of his talent and they moved swiftly to pip the Potteries club to his signature.

Liverpool Echo correspondent Bee was another huge admirer, explaining to his readers that, 'A man of Raisbeck's proportions, style and carriage would rivet attention anywhere. He was a picture at five feet nine inches and fully 12 and a half stone; a fine and beautifully balanced figure.'

A centre-half of repute, but not only in a traditional defensive sense, Raisbeck was also a playmaker who orchestrated those around him. Similar to a modern-day midfielder, he became the central pivot of Watson's team and a firm favourite with supporters.

Given his natural leadership qualities, the captaincy soon came his way and, during the course of an illustrious Anfield career that spanned 11 seasons, so too would plenty of success.

Back row (left to right): *Billy Dunlop, Archie Goldie, Harry Storer (captain), Matt McQueen, General Stevenson, Tom Wilkie.* ***Middle row:*** *Tom Watson (secretary/manager), James Chapman (trainer), Andrew McCowie, Bill Goldie, Raby Howell, Alex Raisbeck, Charlie Wilson, Tom Cleghorn, John McKenna (director).* ***Front row:*** *Bobby Marshall, Johnny Walker, George Allan, Hugh Morgan, Tommy Robertson.*

7. RISE OF THE LIVERS

The shirts are now red – switched in 1896 – and Liverpool have consolidated their position in the top-flight.

It's two years into Tom Watson's managerial reign and, with a squad bolstered by some notable recent arrivals, including Alex Raisbeck, Tommy Robertson, Johnny Walker and George Allan, there are tangible signs that success is brewing.

For this squad of players, the most thrilling season yet in the club's short but eventful history was to come. It began with a resounding 4-0 victory on the opening day and featured a first-ever double over Everton.

There was also another exciting FA Cup run and, come March 1899, genuine talk that the 'Livers' – as they were often referred to in the press – could pull off a league and cup double.

8. UP FOR THE CUP

The Liverpool team line up in the goalmouth at Burnden Park, Bolton, ahead of the 1899 FA Cup semi-final replay against Sheffield United.

This was the second instalment of an epic tie that would go down in the competition's history as one of the most incident-packed and controversial.

The first game had finished 2-2 and excitement was at fever pitch when the teams met again for the right to play Derby County in the final.

As tension builds ahead of kick-off, the Liverpool players casually pose for a pre-match picture. They appear relaxed and have a look of determination etched across their faces.

Unfortunately, what unfolds over the course of the next 90 minutes will have left some of them mentally scarred for a long time.

Twice Liverpool took a two-goal lead and twice they were pegged back with the game finishing 4-4. It was a missed opportunity of massive proportions and goalkeeper Harry Storer, distinguishable in the photograph only by his cap, was the fall guy; criticised heavily and subsequently dropped.

The second replay was then abandoned because of a pitch invasion – with Liverpool leading 1-0 at the time – before Sheffield United eventually brought this long-running drama to a close by prevailing at the fourth attempt.

Dreams of a possible double had been dashed and, to complete Liverpool's misery, a month later they also lost to Aston Villa in the title decider.

A season of progress it had been, but a case of so near yet so far.

(Left to right): *Tommy Robertson, Jack Cox, Hugh Morgan, Alex Raisbeck, Johnny Walker, Archie Goldie, Harry Storer, Raby Howell, George Allan, Billy Dunlop, Bill Goldie.*

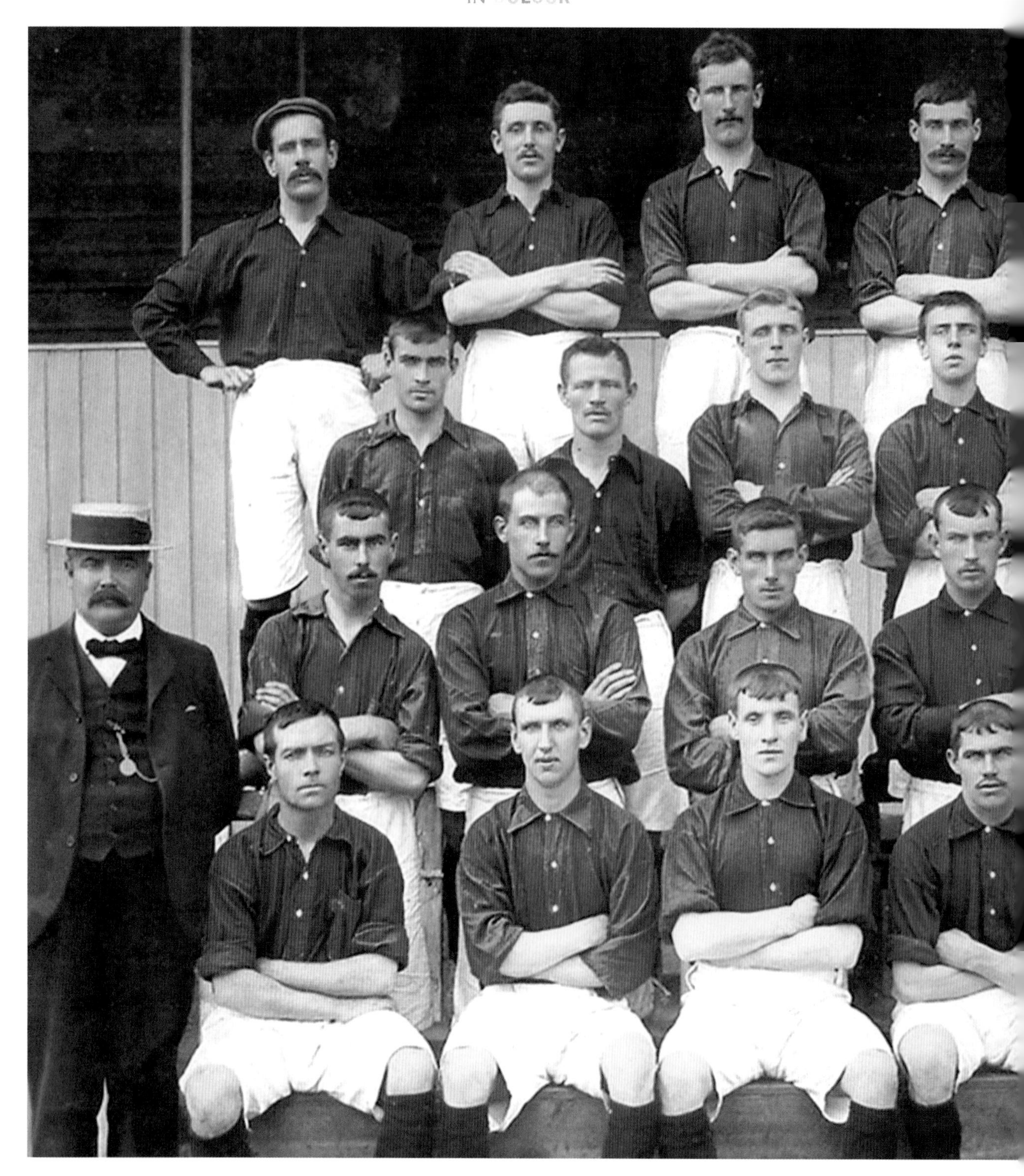

9. NEW CENTURY REDS

This is the team that took Liverpool Football Club into the 20th century.

Fresh from going so close to league and FA Cup glory the previous season, confidence was high as the players regrouped for the annual summer photo-shoot.

That double disappointment, however, would prove difficult to shake off.

Changes in playing personnel had been minimal but Liverpool's fortunes were also undoubtedly hindered by the unexpected loss of George Allan.

A notable absentee on this picture, Allan was suffering with tuberculosis and tragically passed away in October 1899.

His replacement, Peter Kyle, went on to make only five appearances and failed to register a single goal.

At the opposite end, Bill Perkins took over in goal but aspirations of success were ended prematurely.

An eight-game losing sequence early in the season put paid to a title challenge, while interest in the FA Cup went no further than a second-round replay.

But, as the saying goes, 'form is temporary, class is permanent' and despite the 1899/00 season being written off as a huge anti-climax, glory was not far off.

Back row (left to right): *Harry Storer, Billy Dunlop, Bill Perkins, Archie Goldie, General Stevenson.* ***Third row:*** *Bill Goldie, Raby Howell, Alex Raisbeck, Fred Uttley, Charlie Wilson.* ***Second row:*** *Tom Watson (secretary/manager), Jack Cox, John Walker, Tom Robertson, Peter Kyle, Rob McLaren, James Chapman (trainer).* ***Front row:*** *Fred Geary, John Hunter, Hugh Morgan, Abraham Foxall, David Wilson.*

TROPHY HUNTERS...1900-14

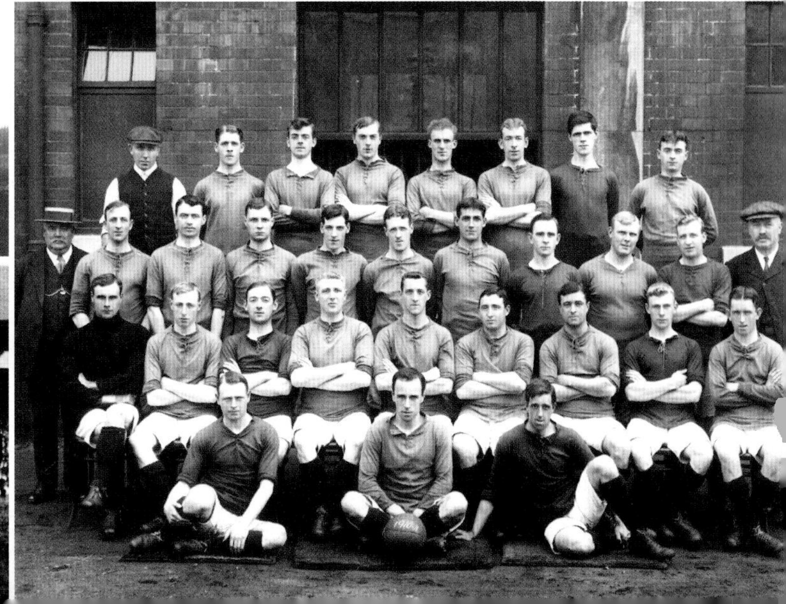

10. CONQUERING HEROES

The newly-crowned league champions pose ceremoniously in a local photographic studio to commemorate the most momentous season yet in the history of Liverpool Football Club.

On 29 April 1901, a single goal victory away to West Bromwich Albion saw Liverpool confirmed as the undisputed best team in the country for the first time.

It had been a title win that set the standard for the generations that followed and the style in which it was achieved was to become a trademark of future Anfield champions.

As late as mid-February, the Reds had been seemingly out of the race, languishing mid-table and nine points adrift of the leaders.

By the time they travelled to the Midlands on the final day of the season, an impressive late surge in form meant they needed only a draw to overtake Sunderland at the top.

A Johnny Walker goal after 20 minutes was enough to complete the job and ensure the First Division championship was heading to Anfield.

The victorious Liverpool team returned to Central Station later that evening where thousands of fans lined the streets to greet them, and a band provided the perfect soundtrack to the moment with a rousing rendition of 'The Conquering Hero'.

The players and directors eventually made their way back to John Houlding's Sandon Hotel by horse-drawn carriage and a night of celebration commenced.

It had been a meteoric ascent to the top for a club that had joined the Football League only eight years before and these are the men that made history.

Captained by the inspirational Alex Raisbeck and with another future Anfield legend, Sam Raybould, topping the scoring charts, this was a Liverpool team of the highest quality.

Look closely at the picture though and there is something rather special missing from the scene.

The trophy on display is not the Football League championship but the Liverpool Senior Cup, won just four days prior to the title being clinched.

The actual date of this photograph and when the official handover of the trophy took place remain unknown.

Back row (left to right): *William Otty, John Glover, Andy McGuigan, Alex J Forrester, John 'Sailor' Hunter, Thomas John Hunter, Raby Howell.*
Middle row: *Tom Soulsby, Charlie Wilson, Sam Raybould, Tommy Robertson, Bill Perkins, Archie Goldie, Maurice Parry, James Chapman (trainer).*
Front row: *Johnny Walker, Billy Dunlop, Alex Raisbeck (captain), Jack Cox, Tom Robertson.*

PECiALS BY OLYMPIAN

11. THIS WAS ANFIELD

This is Liverpool's home ground circa 1903, as it would have looked from what was then known as the Oakfield Road End or Walton Breck Embankment.

On the left is the main 'Grandstand', constructed in 1894, while directly ahead is the recently-rebuilt Anfield Road enclosure.

Note that the building in the corner of the picture would have faced out across Anfield Road towards 'Stanley House', the former home of John Houlding.

Judging by the state of the pitch, the absence of goals and the ladder in front of the fence in the foreground, it appears this picture was probably taken during the summer months.

Improvements off the pitch were in keeping with the impressive progress being made on it and reflected the growing stature of the club.

Although crowds at Anfield had touched 30,000, especially for derby games, the official capacity at this time was believed to be somewhere around 25-28,000, with attendance figures generally averaging out at about 15,000.

A trip to Goodison Park may have still been the bigger draw among local football enthusiasts, but the younger of the city's two clubs was gaining in popularity all the time and would continue to do so.

Back row (left to right): *Sam Hardy, Harry Griffiths, Maurice Parry, Robert Blanthorne, Charlie Wilson, Percy Saul, James Bradley.*
Middle row: *William Connell (trainer), Sam Raybould, Alex Raisbeck, Joe Hewitt, James Hughes, James Gorman, Bobby Robinson, Billy Dunlop, Fred Brown, Ned Doig.*
Front row: *George Latham, Tom Chorlton, John Carlin, Jack Parkinson.*

12. VICTORY SHIELD

Of all the trophies ever won by Liverpool, the award for the biggest – in terms of sheer size – must surely belong to the one that takes pride of place on this team photograph from 1906.

Standing tall at over six foot, it is the Dewar Sheriff of London Charity Shield, the forerunner of the FA Charity Shield.

It was contested annually between 1898 and 1907 by the top professional and amateur sides of the time.

Having been crowned Football League champions for a second time in 1906 Liverpool were duly invited to play the famous Corinthians at Fulham's Craven Cottage and Joe Hewitt netted three times in a 5-1 victory.

The other trophy on display in this picture is

the Liverpool Senior Cup, clinched two days later to complete another memorable season for a club that had bounced back from the shock of relegation in 1904 to reclaim its crown as the best in the country.

The Dewar Shield no longer features on the club's official honours list but at the time there was a lot of prestige attached to it. Between 1935 and 1938 it was even considered, alongside other trophies won by the team, worthy of recognition on the front cover of the matchday programme.

As for hat-trick hero Hewitt, he finished the 1905/06 season as Liverpool's top scorer with 24 goals and, after retiring as a player in 1911, went on to serve the club in a variety of roles for another 60 years.

Back row (left to right): *James Bradley, Bobby Robinson, Jimmy Harrop, Sam Hardy, Tom Chorlton, Tom Rogers, William Connell (trainer).*

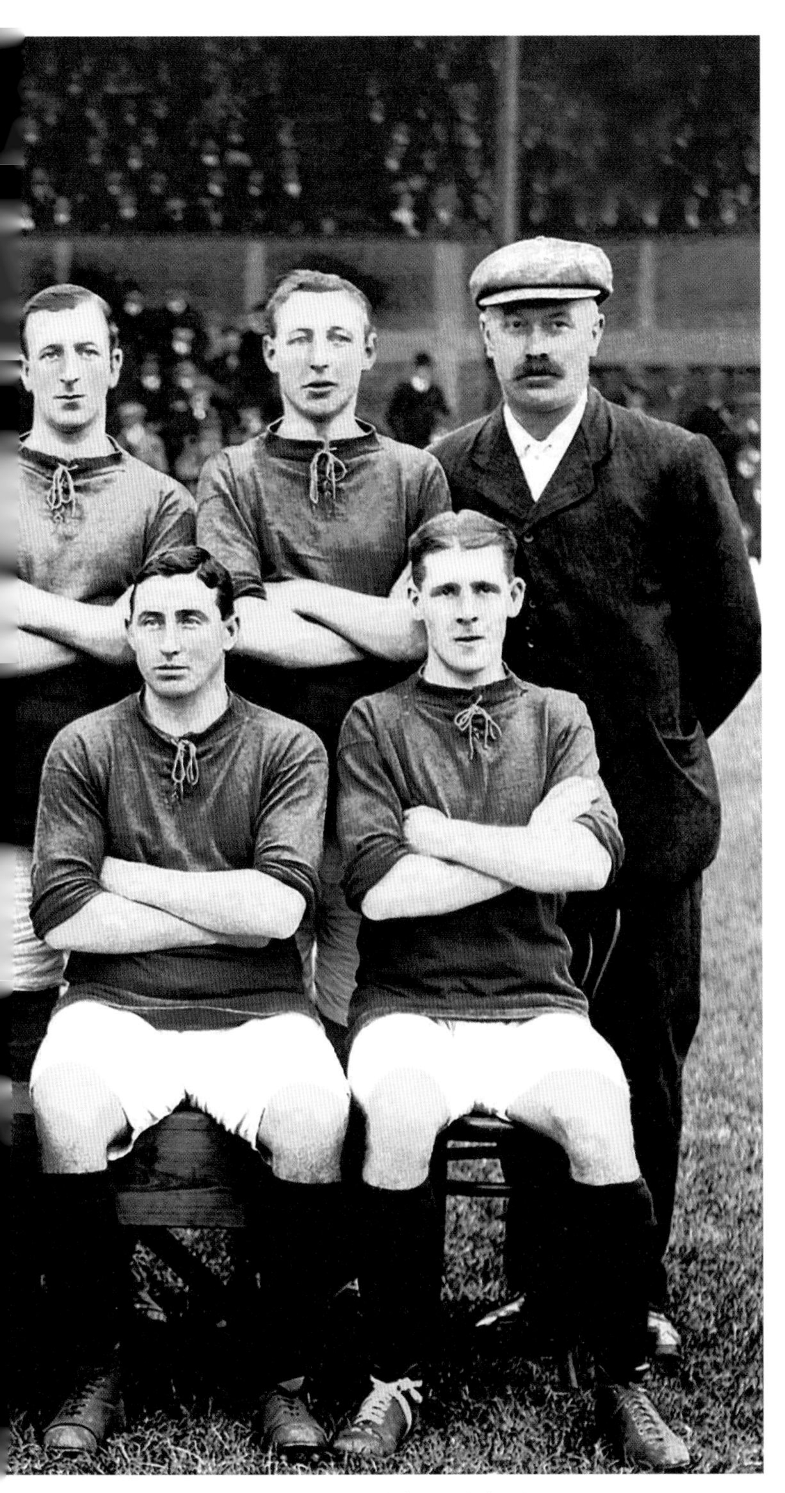

Front row: *Arthur Goddard (captain), Jimmy Stewart, Jack Parkinson, Ronald Orr (vice-captain), John McDonald.*

13. THE RAISBECK-LESS REDS

It's 11 September 1909 and the dawn of a new era at Anfield as the team are snapped prior to the first home game of the season.

Following a narrow escape from relegation just a few months earlier, it had been a summer of change at the club.

For the first time in 15 years there is no Alex Raisbeck in the picture. He, along with several other title-winning stalwarts, has finally moved on.

Fellow hall of famer 'Graceful' Arthur Goddard is now the captain, while Bootle-born Jack Parkinson is set to enjoy his most prolific season in a red shirt.

It was Parkinson who completed the scoring in a 3-1 victory over Blackburn Rovers on the day this photograph was taken, the other two coming from new signings John McDonald and Jimmy Stewart, who netted their first goals for the club in front of a 25,000 crowd.

Despite a lack of pre-season optimism, this was to be a much-improved campaign for the Reds, with the blow of a first hurdle exit in the FA Cup cushioned by a surprising second-place finish in the league.

Tom Chorlton was an ever-present, while Parkinson topped the First Division scoring charts, becoming only the second player in Liverpool history to register 30 goals in a season.

14. EMERGING YOUNGSTERS

The Liverpool squad gather outside the Main Stand for the official photo shoot ahead of the 1910/11 season.

New faces included striker Sam Gilligan, who later scored on his debut, plus two youngsters who would have a big role to play at the club for years to come, Ephraim Longworth and Don McKinlay.

Veteran full-back Billy Dunlop, now in his 15th year at Anfield, is pictured as a Liverpool player for the final time, while fellow full-back Alf West, a 1906 title winner, had returned to the club during the summer but would make only four appearances in his second stint with the Reds.

After finishing runners-up to champions Aston Villa the previous season, hopes were high for the season ahead, yet Liverpool alarmingly slumped to 13th place.

More disappointing at the time though will have been the defeat to neighbours Everton in the second round of the FA Cup.

Bobby Robinson was the only ever-present, while Jack Parkinson once again top scored, this time netting 20 in all competitions.

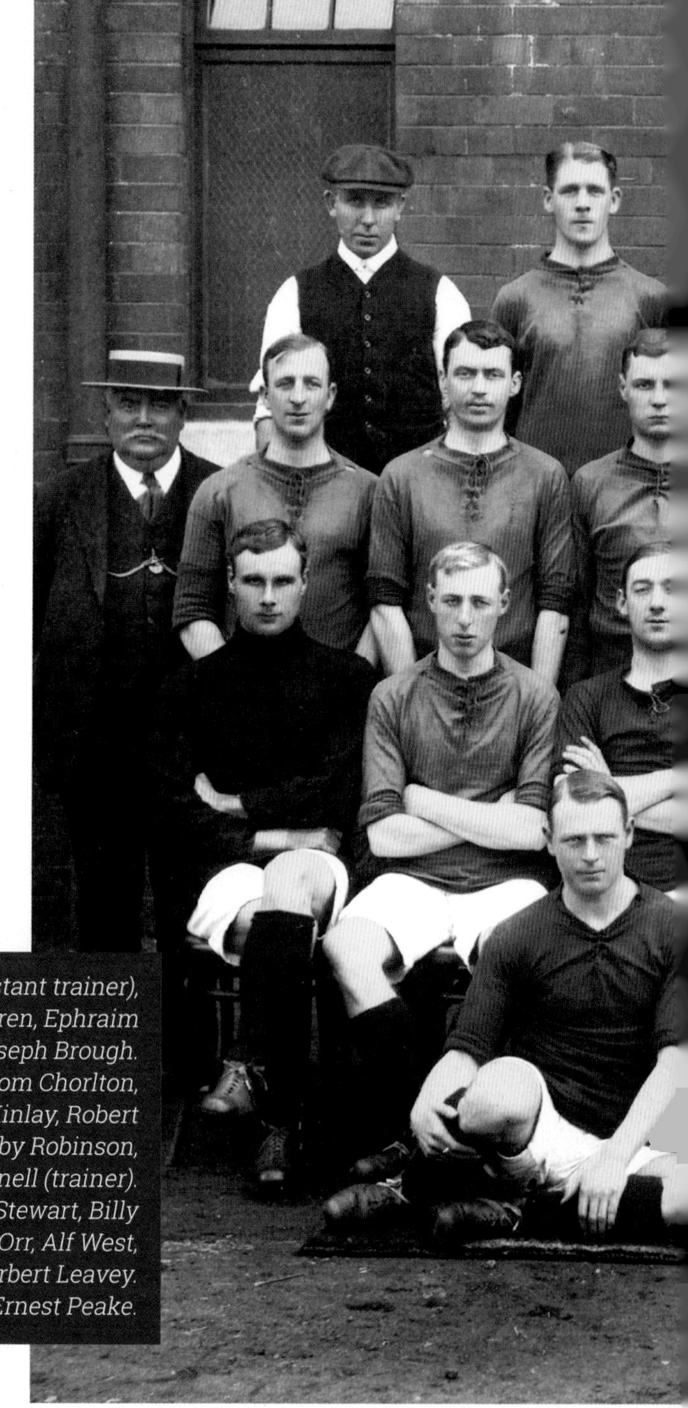

Back row (left to right): *George Fleming (assistant trainer), John McDonald, Peter Malone, Harold Uren, Ephraim Longworth, Samuel Gilligan, James Dillon, Joseph Brough.* ***Middle row:*** *Tom Watson (manager), Tom Chorlton, James Bradley, Augustus Beeby, Don McKinlay, Robert Crawford, Jimmy Harrop, Samuel Hignett, Bobby Robinson, John McConnell, William Connell (trainer).* ***Front row:*** *Sam Hardy, Tom Rogers, James Stewart, Billy Dunlop, Arthur Goddard, Ronald Orr, Alf West, John Speakman, Herbert Leavey.* ***On the ground:*** *Sam Bowyer, Jack Parkinson, Ernest Peake.*

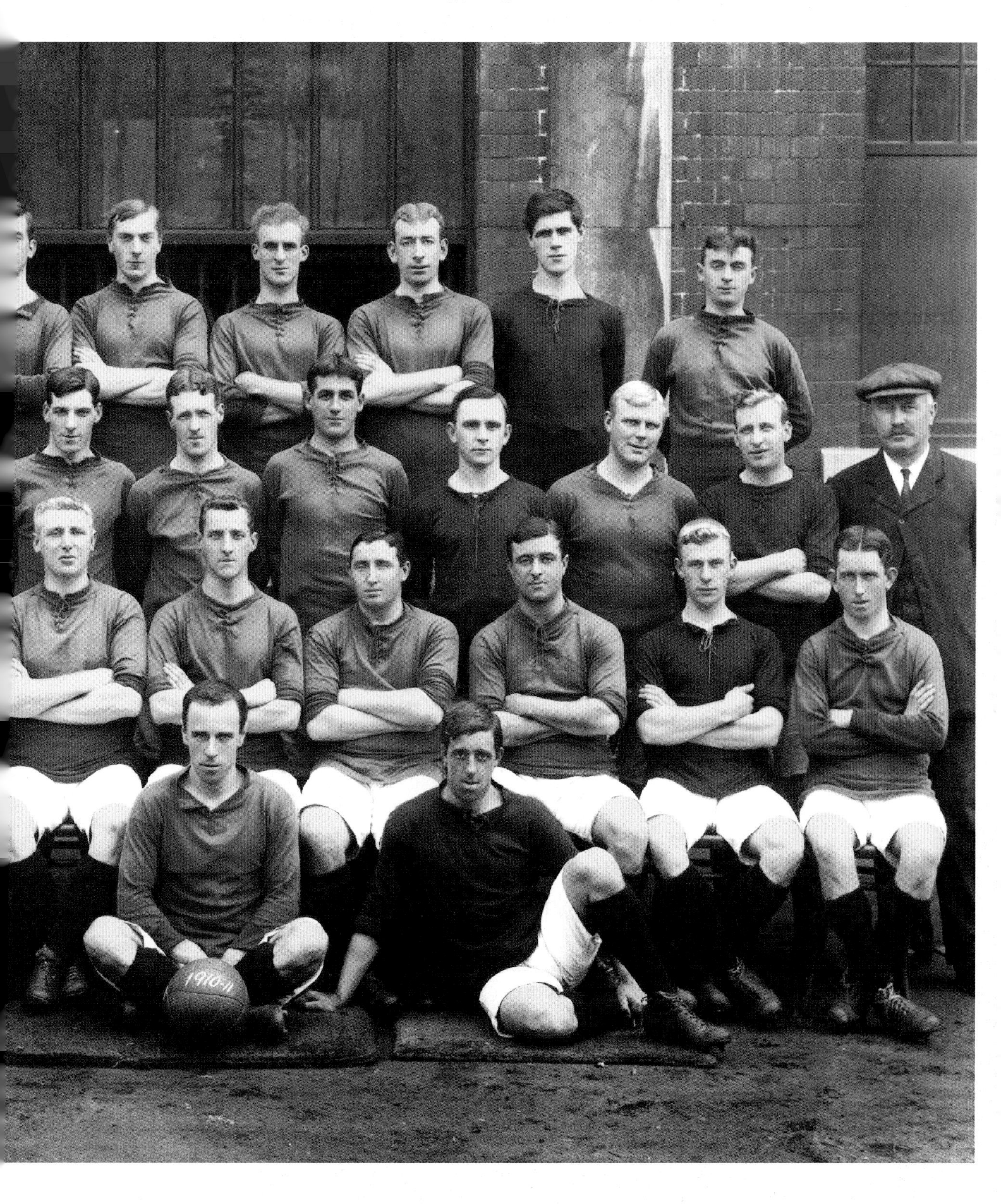
1910-11

15. BUILDING BLOCKS

Highly respected trainer Bill Connell takes on the role of senior figure in the absence of manager Tom Watson as the players gather for the annual squad photograph in 1911/12.

Among the notable new arrivals for the season ahead are Kenneth Campbell, Bob Pursell and Harry Lowe, as the team that would reach the club's first FA Cup final two years later continues to take shape.

For celebrated goalkeeper Sam Hardy, this was to be his last season at the club, while vice-captain and inside-forward Ronald Orr would depart midway through the campaign.

Ephraim Longworth made most appearances, missing just one game, while Jack Parkinson finished top scorer for the third successive season, registering 13 goals.

It would be a season to forget though as Liverpool

narrowly avoided relegation, finishing fourth from bottom and surviving by just a point.

Needing a victory away to fellow strugglers Oldham in their final game to guarantee safety, Sam Gilligan scored the crucial goal after just two minutes.

In the FA Cup it was a familiar story as they once again bowed out early, crashing to a shock 3-0 defeat away to Fulham in just the second round.

Back row (left to right): *Robert Crawford, Ephraim Longworth, Peter Malone, Sam Hardy, Kenneth Campbell, Bob Pursell, Tom Chorlton, Tom Rogers.*
Middle row: *George Fleming (assistant trainer), James Scott, Harry Lowe, Ernest Peake, Jimmy Harrop, Don McKinlay, Bobby Robinson, John McConnell, William Connell (trainer).*
Front row: *John Bovill, Herbert Leavey, James Speakman, Arthur Goddard (captain), Jimmy Stewart, Jack Parkinson, Sam Bowyer, Sam Gilligan, Harold Uren, William Stuart, John McDonald.*
On the ground: *Joe Brough, Henry Beveridge, Ronald Orr (vice-captain), David McDonald.*

16. WELCOME TO THE SPION KOP

Supporters start to congregate early before the turnstiles open...eager to get their 'speck' on the vast open terrace that would soon become such an iconic part of Liverpool's history.

Flat-capped Liverpudlians wait patiently to hand over their sixpence admission fee, while barefooted street urchins mingle freely alongside the young toffs in the growing crowd.

Local ladies take the opportunity to sell their wares and a well-dressed gentleman crosses the tramlines towards what is now the local bakery.

This typical matchday scene at 'flagpole corner', where the mast of Isambard Kingdom Brunel's Great Eastern had stood since the 1890s, is believed to have been captured sometime around 1912, six years after the construction of football's most famous home end.

The club's ever-increasing popularity in the early years of the 20th century necessitated the need for a bigger capacity to meet the demand.

During the summer of 1906 a massive rebuilding project began, planned and overseen by esteemed Glasgow-based engineer Archibald Leitch.

The result of this ambitious redesign was an arena befitting the twice champions of England.

Anfield was also now completely walled-in and the ornate cast-iron sign to the left of the picture let passers-by know exactly where they were – at one of the finest sporting venues in the country.

It included a new Main Stand, constructed with a revolutionary reinforced concrete base and the new elevated terrace, the outside of which we see here.

Consisting of 132 tiered steps, it towered over the rest of the ground, could house up to 20,000 spectators and would soon be christened the Spion Kop.

HALF TIME
PASS OUT
HALF TIME
3d
6d
6d
6d

17. CAPITAL GAINS

Ephraim Longworth and Harry Lowe combine to thwart a Chelsea attack at a sparsely populated Stamford Bridge on 9 September 1912.

In a game that kicked off at 5pm on a Monday evening, Joe Dines made his Liverpool debut in front of a 16,000 crowd as the Reds recovered from a poor start to claim their third straight victory of the season.

Angus Douglas had put the hosts ahead in the 16th minute, but Arthur Goddard equalised shortly after the break and, with time almost up, Tom Gracie headed home a Bill Lacey cross to snatch the points.

Match-winner Gracie had been signed from Everton, along with Lacey, earlier that year and this was his second goal for the club.

FOOTBALL
OFFICIAL
PROGRAMME

NINTH YEAR

Great Concession. During January only.

Suits to Measure
26/6
7/6 Trousers 7/6

First-rate Materials
Sound Workmanship
Excellent Trimmings
and an Assured Fit

The Whole Stock shown in the Windows
ONE PRICE ONLY

BEATY BROS. Ltd. The Celebrated Tailors

ONLY Addresses: London Road & Church Street, LIVERPOOL

ROYAL HIPPODROME. TWICE NIGHTLY AT 6-50 & 9.

LIVERPOOL FOOTBALL CLUB FIXTURES.

FIRST TEAM. 1912-1913. FIRST TEAM.

DATE	NAME OF CLUB	GOALS F	GOALS A	GOALS Pts.		Where Played
1912.						
Sept. 4	Oldham Athletic	[illegible]	[illegible]	[illegible]	L	Home
" 7	Woolwich Arsenal	[illegible]	[illegible]	[illegible]	L	Home
" 9	Chelsea	[illegible]	[illegible]	[illegible]	L	Away
" 14	Bradford City	[illegible]	[illegible]	[illegible]	L	Away
" 21	Manchester City	[illegible]	[illegible]	[illegible]	L	Home
" 28	W. Brom. Albion	[illegible]	[illegible]	[illegible]	L	Away
Oct. 5	Everton	[illegible]	[illegible]	[illegible]	L	Home
" 12	Sheffield Wed.	[illegible]	[illegible]	[illegible]	L	Away
" 14	Sheffield United	[illegible]	[illegible]	[illegible]	L	Away
" 19	Blackburn Rovers	[illegible]	[illegible]	[illegible]	L	Home
" 26	Derby County	[illegible]	[illegible]	[illegible]	L	Away
Nov. 2	Tottenham H'spur	[illegible]	[illegible]	[illegible]	L	Home
" 9	Middlesbrough	[illegible]	[illegible]	[illegible]	L	Away
" 16	Notts County	[illegible]	[illegible]	[illegible]	L	Home
" 23	Manchester U.	[illegible]	[illegible]	[illegible]	L	Away
" 30	Aston Villa	[illegible]	[illegible]	[illegible]	L	Home
Dec. 7	Sunderland	[illegible]	[illegible]	[illegible]	L	Away
" 14	Bolton Wanderers	[illegible]	[illegible]	[illegible]	L	Away
" 21	Sheffield U.	[illegible]	[illegible]	[illegible]	L	Home
25	Oldham Athletic	[illegible]	[illegible]	[illegible]	L	Away
" 26	Newcastle United	[illegible]	[illegible]	[illegible]	L	Home
" 28	Woolwich Arsenal	[illegible]	[illegible]	[illegible]	L	Away

DATE.	NAME OF CLUB.	GOALS F	GOALS A	GOALS Pts.		Where Played
1913.						
Jan. 1	Newcastle United	[illegible]	[illegible]	[illegible]	L	Away
" 4	Bradford City	[illegible]	[illegible]	[illegible]	L	Home
" 11	E.C. Tie	[illegible]	[illegible]	[illegible]		Home
" 18	Manchester City	[illegible]	[illegible]	[illegible]	L	Away
" 25	W. Brom. Albion	[illegible]	[illegible]	[illegible]		Home
Feb. 1	E.C. Tie	[illegible]	[illegible]	[illegible]		
" 8	Everton	[illegible]	[illegible]	[illegible]	L	Away
" 15	Sheffield Wed.	[illegible]	[illegible]	[illegible]	L	Home
22	Blackburn R. E.C.	[illegible]	[illegible]	[illegible]	L	Away
Mar. 1	Derby County	[illegible]	[illegible]	[illegible]	L	Home
" 8	Tottenham H. E.C.	[illegible]	[illegible]	[illegible]	L	Away
" 15	Middlesbrough	[illegible]	[illegible]	[illegible]	L	Home
" 21						
" 22	Notts County	[illegible]	[illegible]	[illegible]	L	Away
" 24	Chelsea	[illegible]	[illegible]	[illegible]	L	Home
" 29	Manchester U. E.C.	[illegible]	[illegible]	[illegible]	L	Home
Apl. 5	Aston Villa	[illegible]	[illegible]	[illegible]	L	Away
" 12	Sunderland	[illegible]	[illegible]	[illegible]	L	Home
" 19	Bolton Wan. EC.	[illegible]	[illegible]	[illegible]	L	Home

English Cup.—Competition Proper Jan. 11th, Feb. 1st and 22nd, Mar. 8th and 29th, April 19th.

A matchday programme and fixture card from the 1912-13 season

But while Lacey would have a significant role to play in the club's future success, Gracie was soon dropped from the team and, after returning to his native Scotland, sadly died of Leukaemia just three years later.

As for Liverpool's fortunes in the aftermath of this match, their promising start came to an abrupt halt with a run of six straight defeats.

Mixed results, including some heavy defeats, saw them eventually finish in mid-table, on the same points as Everton.

This season was the first of two stints Longworth would have as skipper. Lowe succeeded him at the start of the following campaign and, but for injury, should have been the first man to lead the team out in an FA Cup final.

HERWIN'S MOTOR GARAGE
WILLIAM STREET
WOOLWICH
BOVRIL
BUCH

18. SHOOTING DOWN THE GUNNERS

Liverpool inside-forward Arthur Metcalf terrorises the Woolwich Arsenal defence during an emphatic FA Cup success for the Reds in February 1913.

At a waterlogged Manor Ground in Plumstead, there was no stopping Metcalf on this memorable afternoon – despite the atrocious conditions and the close attention of five defenders.

Signed from Newcastle just four months earlier, the clever north easterner opened the scoring after 25 minutes. Bill Lacey added a second before the Gunners pulled a goal back, but Metcalf then went on to complete an impressive hat-trick, netting in the 66th and 82nd minutes to seal Liverpool's place in the next round.

The 4-1 victory was described in that evening's *Football Echo* as 'an easy win' but Liverpool's FA Cup run was to go no further than the next stage, when defeated by Newcastle 1-0 in a replay, following a 1-1 draw at Anfield.

Metcalf finished the season as the club's top scorer, with a prolific strike rate of 18 goals in 32 games and would play a key role the following season when Liverpool reached the FA Cup final for the first time.

After hanging up his boots he worked as a gate man at Anfield but fell ill following a game against Sunderland in February 1936 and passed away, aged just 46, at his home in nearby Stanley Park Avenue a few days later.

19. CHARLIE BUCHAN'S FOOTBALL MASTERCLASS

A view from the Anfield touchline of the First Division fixture between Liverpool and Sunderland on 12 April 1913.

For Liverpool it was nothing more than a routine end-of-season run-out. Interest in the chase for honours had long gone, but for the table-topping visitors it was a must-win match.

Five months earlier, Sunderland centre-forward Charlie Buchan had almost single-handedly destroyed Liverpool, scoring five in a 7-0 rout at Roker Park – and it was to be his day once again.

Here we see the Reds launching an attack towards the Anfield Road end but by half-time Buchan had already netted twice – his second being described by the *Echo* as 'the best seen on this ground for many a day' – and the champions-elect led 4-0.

According to the Athletic News, 'With head and feet Buchan was irresistible; he made the football easy for his comrades, while the shots he sent in were terrific.'

Ten minutes from the end he completed his hat-trick before Arthur Metcalf pulled two late goals back to slightly ease Liverpool's shame.

The team in stripes duly wrapped up the title a week later while Buchan continued to be a thorn in Liverpool's side for the remainder of his career, registering a record 21 goals against them in just 27 games.

Credit where credit is due.

20. PLAY UP LIVERPOOL

FA Cup fourth round action from January 1914 saw Liverpool's continuing crusade to reach the final for a first time gather pace once again.

After defeating Barnsley in the opening round, Gillingham are the visitors to Anfield and, although ex-Red Sam Gilligan was their player-manager, the then Southern League club were something of an unknown quantity.

To date, this is the only ever meeting between the two clubs and our photograph shows Gilligan challenging for the ball with Scottish half-back Bob Ferguson.

It was a tie of huge interest and the intrigue to see these 'mystery men' from Kent drew the biggest crowd of the season yet to Anfield.

On a windy afternoon, over 42,000 witnessed a keenly fought contest, in

which the minnows put up a brave fight before ultimately succumbing to two late goals.

The home fans were forced to wait until the 81st minute before seeing the deadlock broken and it was Irishman Bill Lacey who delivered with a long-range drive.

It was a goal that broke the visitors' dogged resistance and within another couple of minutes Liverpool had doubled their advantage through Ferguson.

The final score suggests a place in the fifth round had been comfortably secured but it was a hard-fought victory.

Nevertheless, it left Liverpudlians dreaming once more that this could be their year and, although there would be a late twist in that tale, the Reds went on to progress further in the competition than ever before.

WR

21. LONDON CALLING

FA Cup final day in 1914 saw these Liverpudlians heading through the streets of the capital to cheer on their team in English football's showpiece event for the first time ever.

Since defeating Aston Villa in the semi-final a month earlier, excitement levels had reached fever pitch and all roads now led to the Crystal Palace ground in Sydenham that would host this historic occasion against Burnley.

Despite the increasing threat of war, 12 special trains had left Lime Street on Friday evening and, 'in the history of local football never have such scenes occurred as these,' reported the Daily Post.

This unprecedented enthusiasm bubbled over into Saturday morning as more supporters filled one of the biggest trains on record for the early football special, transferring 'the population of a village from Liverpool to London in one swoop'.

The travelling red army was estimated to be in excess of 20,000 and they certainly made their presence felt. All were in high spirits and confident that their team could bring the cup home for the first time.

Those pictured here on a horse-drawn carriage were smartly kitted out in the fashionable match-going attire of the day; overcoats and three-piece suits, not forgetting, of course, their specially made red and white 'cup final' hats and matching button bouquets.

Judging by the look on some of their faces, though, maybe they'd had a premonition of what lay in store.

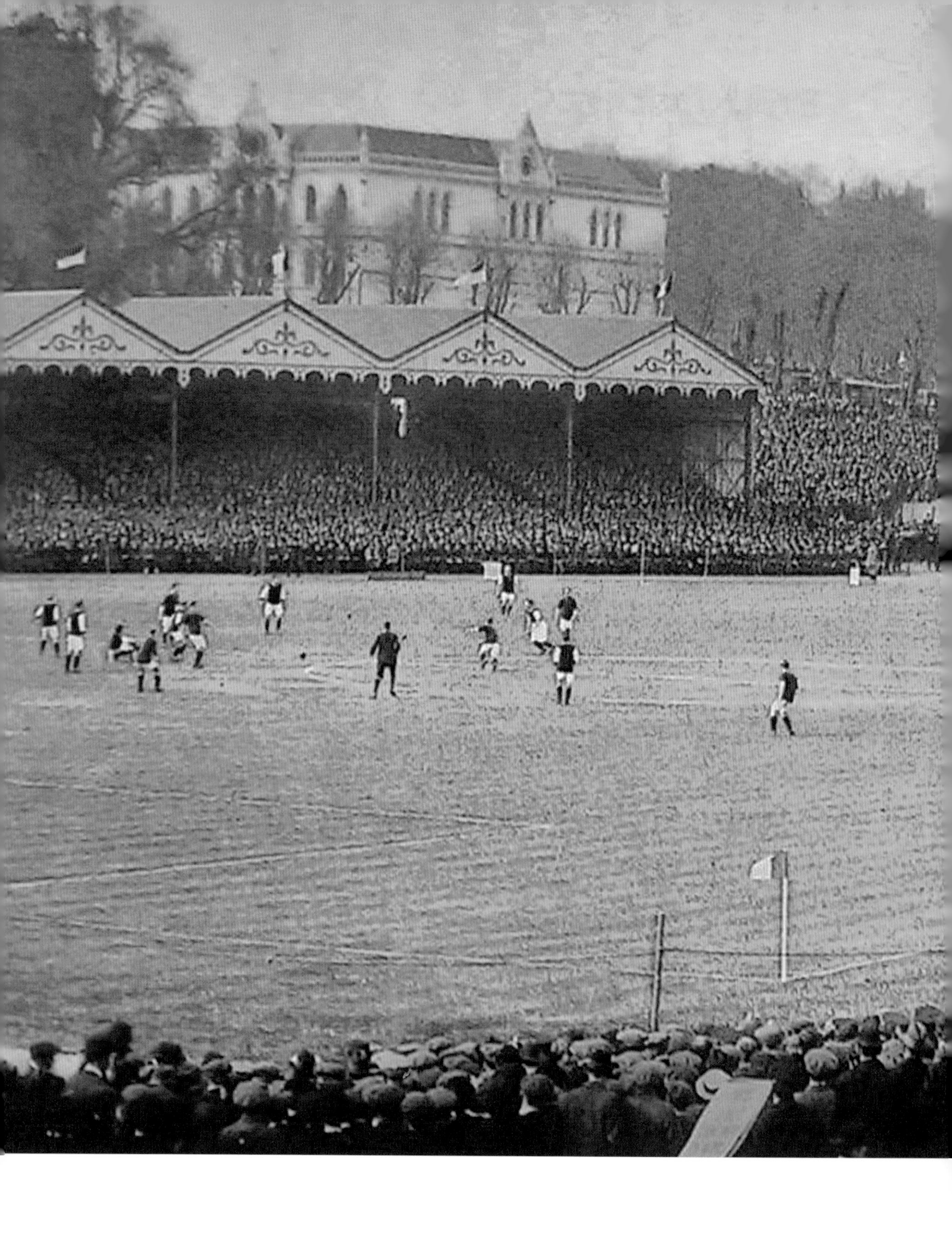

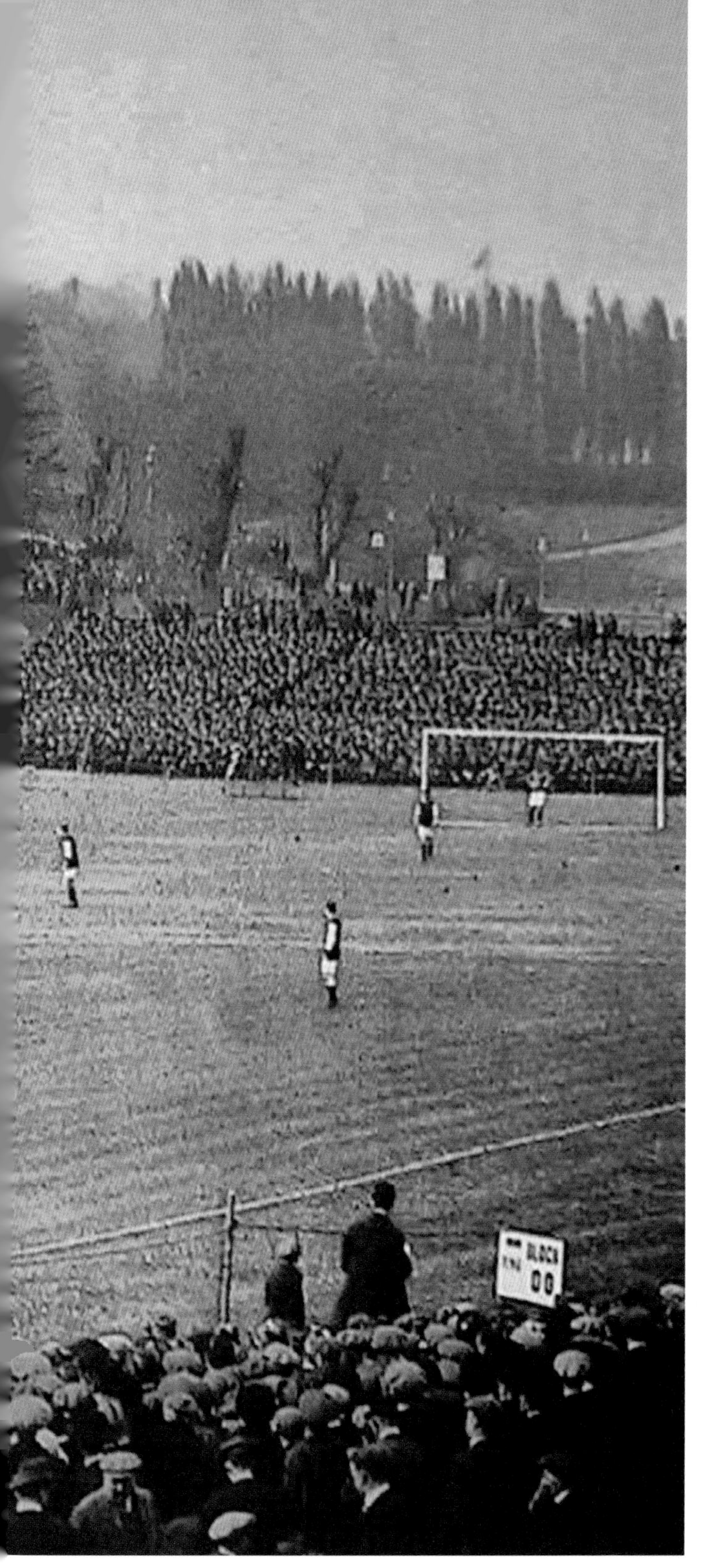

22. CUP OF TEARS AT THE PALACE

A landscape view of what, at the time, was the biggest game in Liverpool's 22-year history, the 1914 FA Cup final at Crystal Palace.

Although the club had already won two league championships, it was the FA Cup that was widely considered to be football's greatest prize; one that captured the imagination of the entire country and was the object of desire for everyone in the game.

If this match wasn't already important enough, the fact that King George V became the first reigning monarch to attend the final made it an even grander occasion.

Liverpool were rated slight favourites but suffered a blow when captain Harry Lowe was sidelined after failing a late fitness test.

On a warm but overcast afternoon, the two teams sported their traditional colours, and despite dominating the first half the Reds unfortunately failed to convert their possession into goals.

After the break Burnley showed signs of improvement and took the lead in the 57th minute with a goal from ex-Everton forward Bert Freeman. It was described as 'good enough to win any game,' and that's exactly what it turned out to be.

Defeat was a bitter blow to Tom Watson and his team, but four days later the finalists met again in a charity match at Anfield and a joint team photograph was taken with the trophy.

It was the closest Liverpool would get to the FA Cup for years. Success in this competition would have to wait – and a long wait it would be.

Left to right: *Jackie Sheldon, Elisha Scott, Walter Wadsworth, Bill Lacey, Ephraim Longworth, Kenneth Campbell, Bob Ferguson, Robert Crawford, Bob McDougall, Arthur Metcalf, Tom Fairfoul.*

23. REDS ON TOUR

This is a Liverpool team with two goalkeepers in the starting line-up during the club's post-season tour of Scandinavia in 1914.

It was only the second time Liverpool had travelled overseas and this trip came hot on the heels of defeat to Burnley in the FA Cup final.

In total, the travelling party would be away for three weeks, and the players are pictured here ahead of their third game of the tour against AIK Solna in Stockholm.

After defeating IFK Goteborg and Djurgarden, the tourists' stock was rising and what was then a record crowd for a club match at this stadium turned out to see what all the fuss was about.

Despite a slow start, blamed on the previous night's lavish hospitality that had been laid on by the Swedish Football Association, the 16,000 in attendance were not disappointed.

The Reds went on to chalk up a third successive victory, going ahead courtesy of an own goal before Bill Lacey and Bob McDougall completed the scoring.

There were another four games to come on the tour, one more in Sweden and three in Denmark, and Liverpool returned home undefeated, winning six and drawing one.

As for the second goalkeeper on this photograph, it was none other than a young Elisha Scott, who took the place of Don McKinlay and played outside-left.

By all accounts he performed well enough, but it was an illustrious career between the sticks that he would ultimately become known for.

24. 'LISHA OF LIVERPOOL

THE ORIGINAL KING OF THE KOP

The legend of Elisha Scott will forever echo at Anfield. Widely regarded as one of football's greatest ever goalkeepers, his remarkable career with the Reds spanned a record-breaking 22 years and he remains one of the most popular figures to have represented the club.

Born in Belfast and signed as a rookie 17-year-old, the younger brother of former Everton 'keeper Billy Scott established himself as Liverpool's undisputed number one in the early Twenties and would be an integral member of the back-to-back title-winning teams.

His fame spread way beyond the confines of L4 but the Irish international's rapport with Kopites of the time was unprecedented and he was the subject of the first reported individual player chant at Anfield.

It was a two-way relationship. Scott would happily chat to supporters while travelling to and from home games and would constantly engage with those who stood behind his goal during matches.

Even when the glory years dried up, Scott's popularity never waned.

A supporter once ran onto the pitch and kissed him after he'd pulled off a stunning save, while there were vehement protests later in his career to stop Liverpool doing the unthinkable and selling him to Everton.

When the day did finally come for him to say goodbye in 1934 it was a sad occasion all round and tears were openly shed on the Kop.

Further proof of Scott's fame would come five years later when a poll was conducted among supporters to determine who had been Liverpool's greatest-ever player and he topped the list.

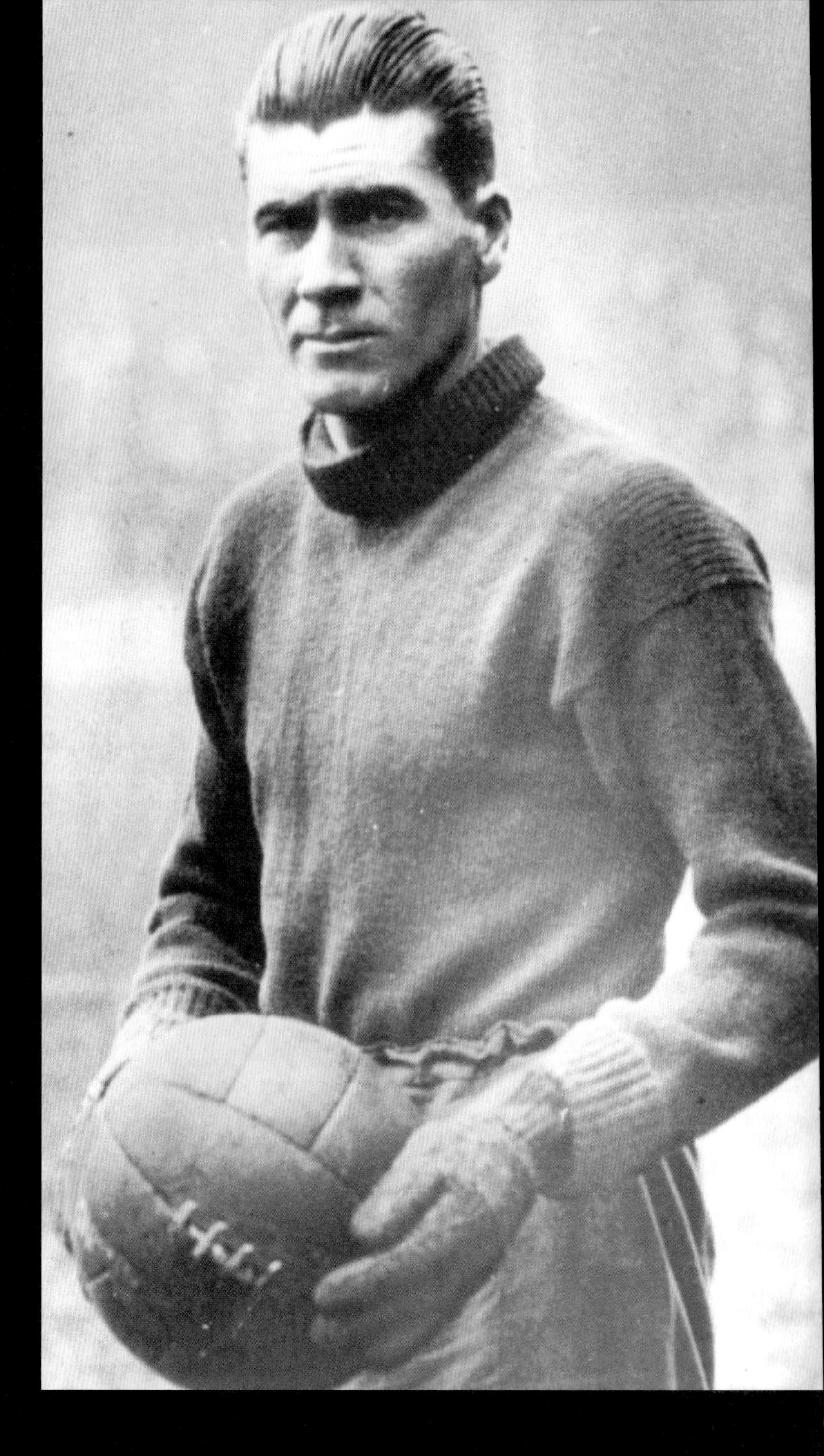

DERBY DAY SPILLS AND THRILLS

The Anfield air is about to turn as blue as the shirts Everton are wearing as confusion reigns in the Liverpool penalty area during the Merseyside derby of October 1922.

Renowned for his expletive-filled tirades during games, Elisha Scott wasn't slow in coming forward if there was something to say and, in his brusque Belfast brogue, he could regularly be heard barking orders and shouting obscenities at those in front of him.

Referees and opposition forwards were often on the receiving end of his wrath, and no-one escaped. Not even his own defenders.

Following the incident captured here, the target of his anger was Reds captain Don McKinlay, whose tame back-pass put him under severe pressure.

As Scott subsequently attempted to clear the danger, an alleged foul by Bobby Irvine went unpunished and William Williams pounced to score from close range.

It was the opening goal of the afternoon, and it stunned the majority inside Anfield, especially as the Reds had started the game top of the First Division, while Everton languished just four places off the bottom.

Luckily for Liverpool, only 17 minutes had elapsed and there was ample time to recover, which they duly did, although the comeback didn't kick in until after the half-time break.

Harry Chambers made history by becoming the first Liverpool player to score a derby hat-trick, Jock McNab, pictured, grabbed a rare goal and Tom Bromilow, on his birthday, added the finishing touch in the final minute.

Liverpool won 5-1. Scott and McKinlay shook hands and made up. The earlier incident had been forgotten. Victory was all that mattered.

SCOTT'S UNITED FRONT

The 'eye of an eagle, swift movement of a panther and clutch of a vice'.

According to one contemporary reporter, these were among the many attributes Elisha Scott possessed.

And, here, on the opening day of the 1926/27 season the Liverpool 'keeper appears to be displaying them all as he successfully defends the Kop goal against Manchester United.

On what was a baking hot late-August afternoon, Don McKinlay and Tom Bromilow look on as Scott comfortably handles a shot from United forward Frank McPherson.

At the opposite end, with winger Dick Edmed shining on his debut, three goals in eight minutes, courtesy of Gordon Hodgson and a Dick Forshaw brace, gave the Reds a commanding first-half lead.

The visitors replied with two goals after the break, both scored by McPherson, but Forshaw went on to complete his hat-trick to make sure of the points.

It had been an impressive start to the season but a day also tinged with sadness following the death of manager Matt McQueen's wife that morning and, as a mark of respect, the Anfield flag was flown at half-mast.

While Scott was never to experience a home defeat at the hands of Manchester United, Forshaw had even more reason to remember games against them.

This was the second successive season that he had netted an Anfield treble at their expense and five months later he was the matchwinner at Old Trafford with what proved to be his final goal for the club.

Elisha Scott attempts to punch the ball clear amid a crowded goalmouth against the team he could have been playing for had his career in England taken a different course at the outset.

It was on New Year's Day 1913 that a teenage Scott made his Liverpool debut in a goalless draw at St James' Park.

And so accomplished was his performance that Newcastle offered £1,000 for his signature immediately afterwards.

Scott was only informed of the bid on the way back to Liverpool and thought it might have been in his best interests to go.

Liverpool's secretary/manager, Tom Watson, fortunately thought otherwise, rejected the offer and reassured Scott that his future lay at Anfield.

As it turned out, Newcastle would be the club he faced on more occasions than any other during the course of his lengthy Liverpool career.

In total, Scott faced the Geordies 25 times so those black and white stripes must have been a familiar sight.

The game he's featured in here ended 1-1. It took place on Valentine's Day 1925 but there was certainly no love lost between the two sides. Jock McNab and Walter Wadsworth (also pictured) were both sent off, as was Tommy Urwin for the visitors.

McNab was dismissed first for kicking an opponent and Wadsworth followed shortly after for punching Urwin, who had thrown mud at him.

The fall-out from the incident rumbled on for weeks and all three were subsequently suspended, Wadsworth for a month and McNab six weeks.

BEST OF ENEMIES. BEST OF FRIENDS

The city's two most famous footballers of the time, Elisha Scott and Dixie Dean, lead out their respective teams at Goodison Park for the 70th Merseyside derby on 1 October 1932.

In recognition of what was to be his 400th league appearance, Scott had been given the honour of captaining the side for only the second time in his lengthy Liverpool career.

It was fitting that it came in a game of this magnitude, providing him with the opportunity to walk out alongside his most famous foe.

The Ulsterman's rivalry with Everton's greatest-ever centre-forward is legendary and their derby day duels will always be part of football folklore on Merseyside.

Friendly off the pitch but competitive on it, the old joke was that if the two met in the street and Dean nodded, Scott would immediately dive across the pavement.

Their presence loomed large over the fixture and would dominate the local sports pages for days either side.

On this occasion, it would be Dean who claimed the bragging rights, netting twice in a 3-1 victory for the Blues after Gordon Gunson, seen here coming out of the tunnel behind Scott, had opened the scoring for Liverpool.

Afterwards, the pair probably met up, as they often did, for a post-match pint in the Lisbon pub on Victoria Street before travelling back to their homes on the Wirral.

Scott was 39 when he played in this game and would appear in just two more derbies before finally returning to his native Belfast in 1934, but left having played more games (468) for the club than any player before him.

THE UNTOUCHABLES...1919-23

25. LFC STARS IN STRIPES

A rare image of Liverpool in an unusual change strip, taken ahead of a First Division fixture at Villa Park in September 1919.

Although never recognised as one of the club's traditional away kit designs, striped shirts were more common than many people think during the years either side of the First World War.

In pre-season trial games, the 'Stripes' often played against the 'Reds', while striped shirts were also worn by combined Liverpool and Everton sides in annual charity games.

The first team also donned stripes for a number of fixtures around this time, notably away to Burnley, Arsenal, Middlesbrough and Manchester United.

What has never been certain though is the colour.

For this match, they were black. It took place just a month into the inaugural season after the war and inside-forward Dick Forshaw, recently signed on a free transfer, netted the first of his 123 goals for the club in a 1-0 win.

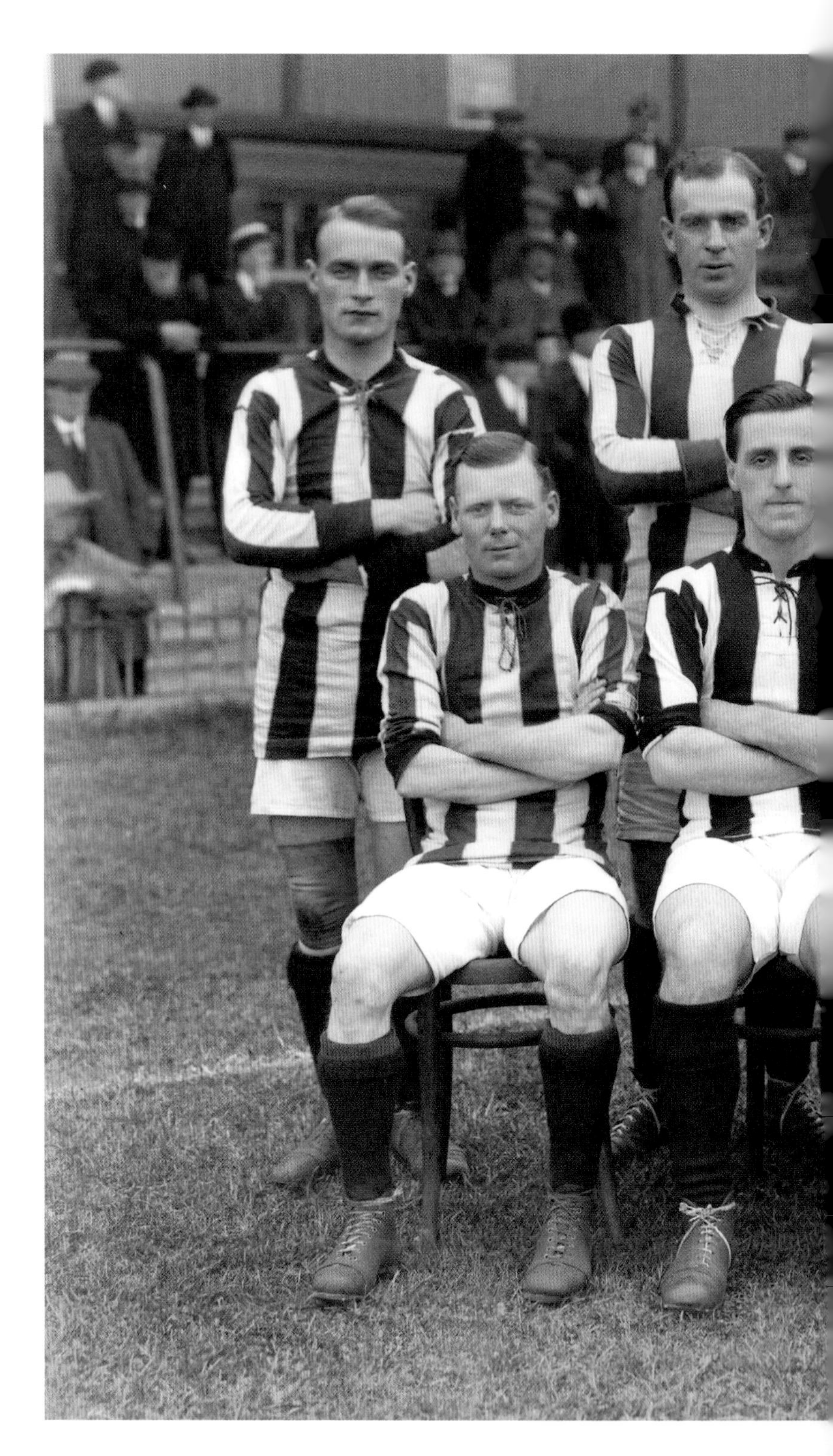

Back row (left to right): *Tommy Lucas, Harry Lowe, Kenneth Campbell, Bill Lacey, Bill Jenkinson, Don McKinlay.*
Front row: *Jackie Sheldon, Harry Chambers, Fred Pagnam, Dick Forshaw, Albert Pearson.*

26. A PRINCE AMONG FULL-BACKS

A study in power, focus, determination, and technique, legendary defender Ephraim Longworth heads the ball clear during a game at Anfield in the 1920s.

One of the most consistent full-backs Liverpool have ever had on their books, Longworth was a club stalwart who had a huge influence on the team that would dominate the First Division in the early part of this decade.

Signed in 1910, his playing career at Anfield was to span a remarkable 18 years, and throughout all this time he served the Reds with nothing but distinction.

He enjoyed two separate spells as captain and was also the first Liverpool player to skipper England, achieving the latter honour in 1921 when aged 33.

With a lock of blond hair hanging over his forehead, Longworth was an instantly recognisable figure whose composed style of play made him a firm favourite with fans and team-mates.

Renowned as being proficient with either foot, his appearances for the Reds eventually totalled 371, and would have been much more had it not been for the war, though famously he was never to score a goal.

By the time he pulled on a red shirt for the final time in 1928, Longworth was just a few months off his 41st birthday and he remained at the club long after hanging up his boots – first as a trusted member of the back-room team and then on the Anfield ground staff. A true club servant.

27. TERRIFIC TRIO

Three Liverpool managers appear in the same photograph alongside the club's directors at an event in the early 1920s.

Between them, George Patterson, Dave Ashworth and Matt McQueen would clock up just over 750 games in charge of the Reds, but there is more to their Anfield careers than mere statistics.

The manager when this picture was taken was Ashworth, a former referee who was recruited from Stockport County in 1919. Within three seasons his team was good enough to be crowned champions, but he suddenly resigned in December 1922 with them on course to repeat the feat.

Amid the turmoil, ex-player and director McQueen stepped into the breach; a steadying hand to ensure the title was retained.

In 1924 he lost a leg after being involved in a car accident but remained as manager until 1928 when ill-health eventually forced him to call it a day.

The board then turned to secretary Patterson, who had served the club since 1908.

Renowned more for his administration skills, Patterson had taken control of team affairs briefly before Ashworth and knew the club inside out.

His second spell at the helm lasted eight years, during which time he helped launch the careers of several future Anfield legends.

What this trio of managers achieved may have since been overshadowed by those who followed in their footsteps, but the part they played in the club's history should never be forgotten.

Back row: *Unidentified.*
Third row: *Walter Cartwright (director), Unidentified, George Patterson (manager).*
Second row: *Harvey Webb (director), Edward Bainbridge (director), Walter Robert Williams (chairman), Robert Martindale (director), John Asbury (vice-chairman).*
Front row: *Tom Crompton (director), Matt McQueen (director), Dave Ashworth (manager), Unidentified.*

Left to right: *Dave Ashworth (manager), John Bamber, Jackie Sheldon, Elisha Scott, Tom Bromilow, Walter Wadsworth, Dick Johnson, Harry Chambers, Don McKinlay, Harold Wadsworth, Tommy Lucas.*
On the floor: *Bill Lacey, Ephraim Longworth, Dick Forshaw.*

28. THE PEOPLE'S TEAM

Against the backdrop of what resembles a cast of extras from the *Peaky Blinders* television series, manager Dave Ashworth and his Liverpool players are photographed prior to the home game with Preston North End in September 1920.

Why the picture was taken on this day, and not before the opening fixture of the season, is unclear. So too is the reason why it was done with the players sitting in front of the Main Stand Paddock, as opposed to the traditional team group style.

But with the crowd so close and a sea of faces looking on, all resplendent in their various forms of headwear, it certainly makes for a unique image.

On a memorable afternoon, Harry Chambers got the scoring underway after eight minutes and Harry Wadsworth, younger brother of Walter, soon doubled the advantage.

By half-time it was 3-0, with Dick Johnson getting his name on the scoresheet, and he later helped himself to another three as Liverpool ran out comfortable 6-0 winners.

In what was his first full season at the club, Johnson averaged a goal every other game until getting injured, while Chambers ended the campaign as Liverpool's top scorer with 24.

Apart from the unfortunate Jackie Sheldon, who suffered a broken leg in April 1921 and never played football again, glory beckoned for this group of players.

29. A RED QUARTET

In their woollen polo-neck training jumpers, four of the Liverpool back line take a well-earned breather to pose for the camera during an Anfield training session.

Jock McNab, Walter Wadsworth, John Bamber and Tom Bromilow had been teammates since the first season after the war and remained so despite the intense competition for places in the starting eleven.

The unfortunate member of this quartet though was right-half Bamber, who played the first four games of the 21/22 season before being struck down with appendicitis.

This eventually led to McNab being given his chance and St Helens-born Bamber struggled to get back in.

Along with local pair Wadsworth and Bromilow, Scotsman McNab then went on to play a key role in the success of the Reds over the next two years.

Although Bamber did figure in both of the Untouchables' title-winning seasons, he missed out on a medal in each due to not making the required number of appearances and eventually left in 1924.

McNab remained at Liverpool for the rest of his playing career, before going into the licensing trade, managing the Jawbone Tavern in Bootle.

Wadsworth moved on to Bristol City in 1926, later working in the haulage business, while Bromilow played on at Anfield until 1930 before a career in management.

Left to right: *Jock McNab, Walter Wadsworth, John Bamber and Tom Bromilow.*

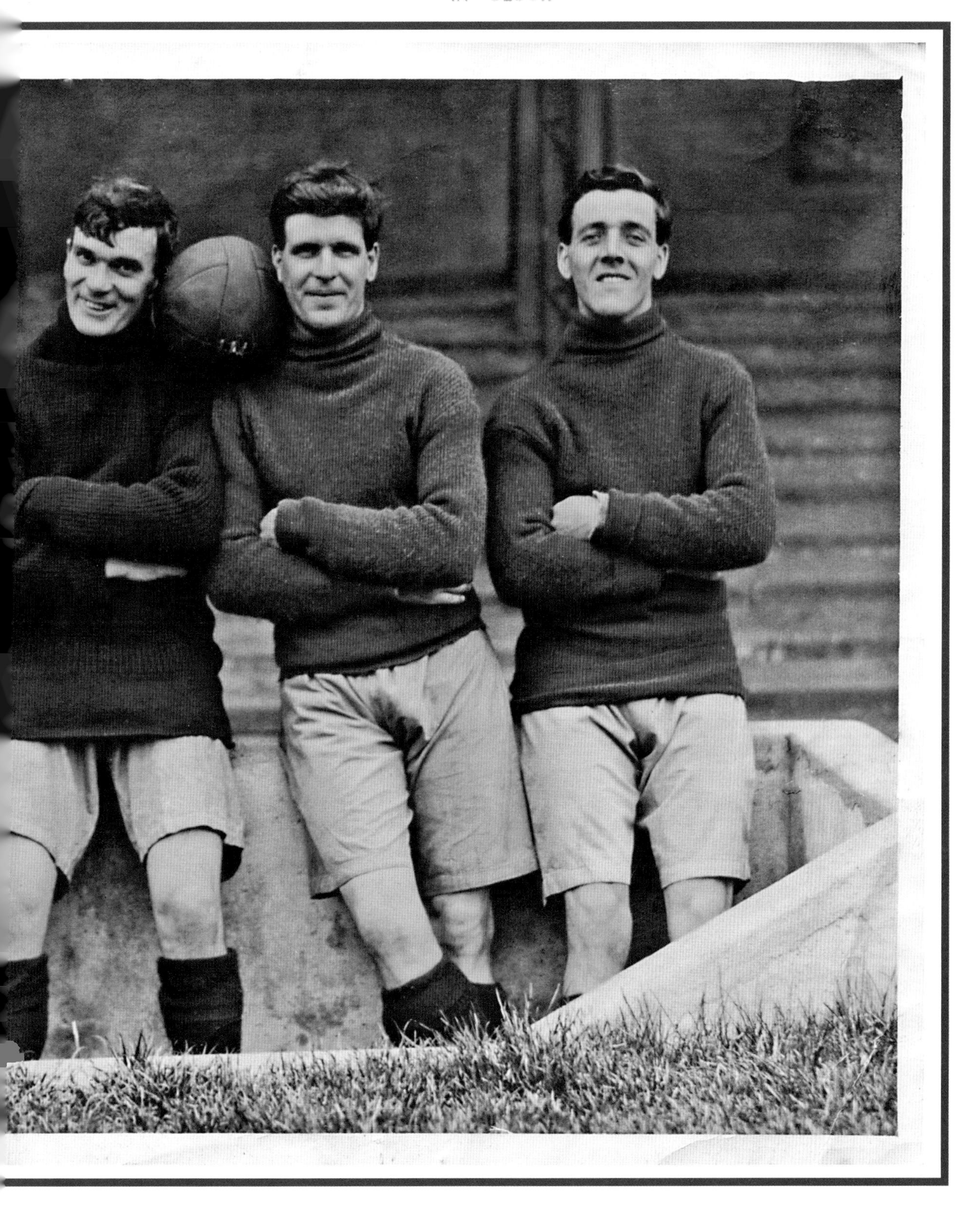

30. ADMIRING THE PRIZE

After an absence of 16 years, an old friend makes a welcome return to Anfield at the close of the 1921/22 season.

Liverpool Football Club are champions of England for a third time, and they now have the silverware to prove it.

The final league table had seen them finish six points clear of nearest challengers Tottenham. Dick Forshaw and Fred Hopkin were ever-presents in the side, while Harry Chambers was top scorer.

Just two defeats in the first 32 league games was the foundation for success and once Liverpool hit top spot in mid-December they never looked back.

The formalities were completed following a 2-1 Easter Monday victory over Burnley, when Chambers and Forshaw scored the goals in front of an exuberant 50,000 home crowd.

The official trophy presentation came a month later and it was made by a familiar face, the now Football League president John McKenna, whose lengthy and illustrious association with the club had come to an end just the previous year. This long-awaited handover ceremony took place on the day of the FA Charity Shield game between the Reds and Huddersfield Town at Old Trafford.

A 1-0 defeat meant the champions missed out on making it a double celebration, but they brought home from Manchester the more important prize.

On the team's return to Exchange Station later that night, captain Don McKinlay was hoisted high onto the shoulders of celebrating supporters who had been waiting to greet them and to get a glimpse of a trophy that had not been in Liverpool hands since 1906.

But before the gleaming 'old lady' was carefully placed back into the Anfield trophy cabinet, it was first perched modestly on an old wooden chair at the side of the Anfield pitch for all to see.

Its presence attracted the admiring glances of some of the players who helped win it, among them half-back Jock McNab, captain Don McKinlay and goalkeeper Elisha Scott.

31. FORZA LIVERPOOL

Still basking in the glow of the acclaim that came their way after being crowned champions, the Liverpool players take to the field in Italy for the start of the 1922 post-season tour.

Milan is their first port of call and the heat is stifling, hence the neck scarves offering protection against sunburn.

But there was no exotic opposition lying in wait for the opening game at the Campo di Viale Lombardia. Instead, it was familiar foes from East Lancashire, Burnley.

Their 'exhibition' match attracted a 10,000 crowd, but given the hot conditions, play was often reduced to walking pace.

The bone-hard playing surface was also not conducive to entertaining football and a drab game was settled in Burnley's favour by a 63rd-minute Bob Kelly goal.

During a week-long stay in Milan the players went on excursions around the Lakes before continuing the tour with further games in Turin, Pisa, Genoa and Vercelli.

Interestingly, the Burnley match was played on 25 May, a date that will forever link Liverpool and Milan, due to events in Istanbul 83 years later.

Left to right: *Cyril Gilhespy, Dick Forshaw, John Bamber, Ephraim Longworth, Walter Wadsworth, Elisha Scott, Don McKinlay, Harry Chambers, Harry Lewis, Bill Lacey, Tom Bromilow.*

32. THE FIELD ON ANFIELD ROAD

A birds-eye view of how Anfield looked in February 1923.

The open Spion Kop terrace is to the bottom left, with Anfield Road and Stanley Park to the top right.

To the left is the famous Archibald Leitch-designed Main Stand, with its iron-framed barrel roof and distinctive red and white mock-Tudor style arched gable centerpiece.

On the opposite side was the original 'Boys Pen'. It had been introduced the previous year and ran along the front of the stand. From the corner flag to just before the halfway line it was capable of housing up to 4,000 young supporters.

Also note the close proximity of the houses on Kemlyn Road that backed directly onto that stand of the same name. It was here, at number 32, that the club's new manager lived.

Just two days before this photograph was taken, director and former player Matt McQueen had been officially installed as successor to Dave Ashworth. He remained a resident in Kemlyn Road throughout his time in charge, and beyond. No Liverpool boss has ever lived closer to his workplace.

Anfield was now capable of holding well over 50,000, with a new record attendance of 54,368 having witnessed the Merseyside derby in October 1922.

Plans for an elaborate triple-decker 'hat-trick' stand at the Anfield Road end, proposed in the early 1920s, never did materialise and the ground looked exactly like this for a further five years until a roof was erected over the Kop in 1928.

33. WE ARE THE CHAMPIONS (AGAIN!)

This is the squad of players that created history in 1922/23 by becoming the first side in almost 20 years to retain the First Division championship.

Not since The Wednesday in 1905 had a team managed to clinch back-to-back league titles but this Liverpool team defied the odds to etch their names into the record books.

Making the achievement even more remarkable was the fact manager Dave Ashworth suddenly resigned midway through the season.

The reasons for him leaving the reigning league champions to join Oldham Athletic, a club languishing near the bottom of Division One, still remain shrouded in mystery, but it failed to knock the Reds off their course to glory.

Nor did two months without a permanent successor in place. By the time Matt McQueen was officially announced as the new boss, Liverpool had opened up a four-point lead at the top.

The title was eventually clinched with two games to spare, courtesy of a 1-1 draw at home to Huddersfield Town in which top scorer Harry Chambers, seen here on the bottom left popping his head through the legs of John Bamber, netted the all-important goal.

Notable absentees on this photograph include Tom Bromilow, Elisha Scott, Don McKinlay and Ephraim Longworth, but everyone was keen to get their hands on the prize once again, and with good reason.

It would be another 54 years before a Liverpool team successfully defended the league championship.

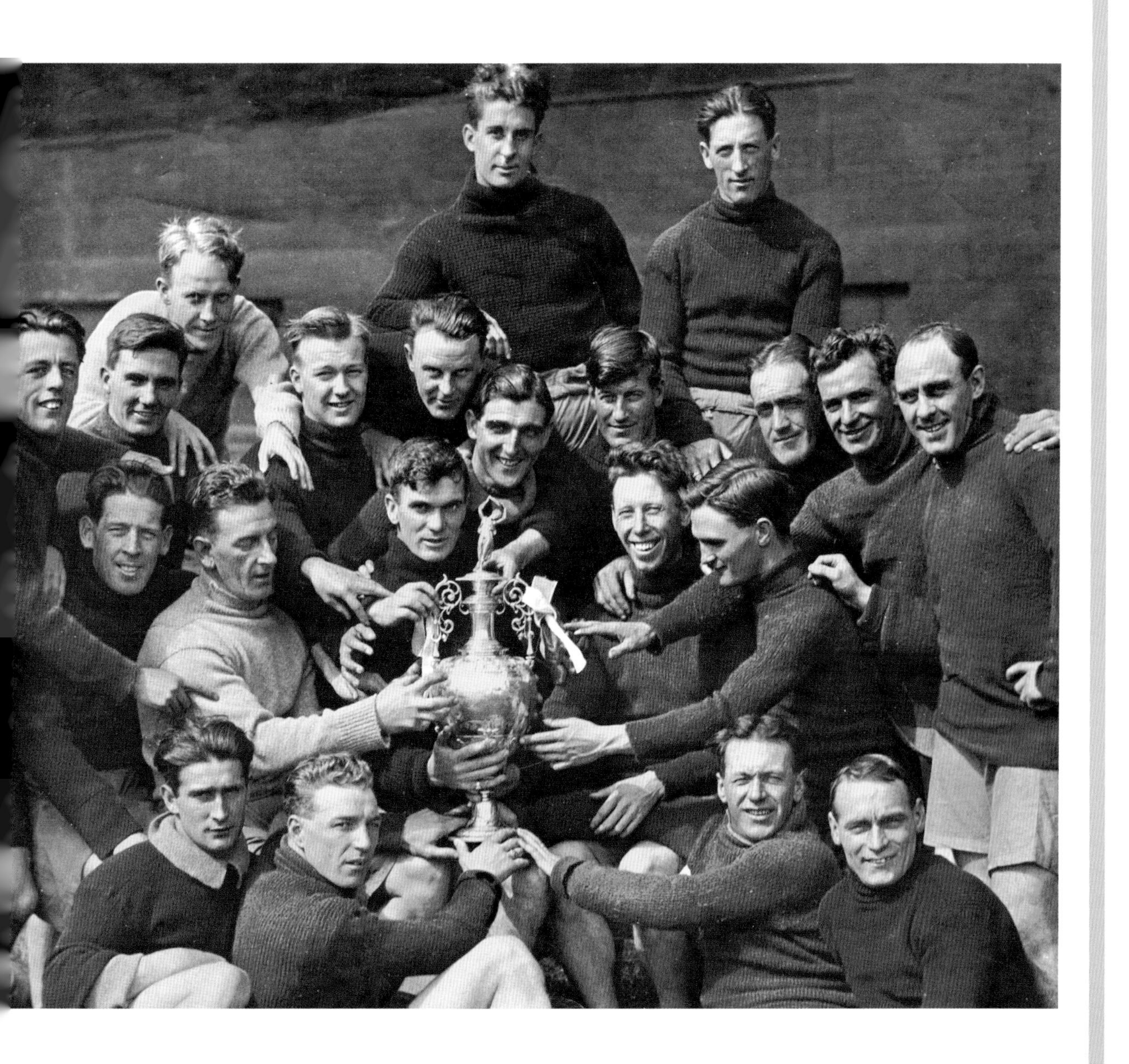

34. REG THE RED

THE LIVERPOOL BOYS ARE IN TOWN

A merry band of travelling Liverpudlians make a brief pit-stop in Trafalgar Square while en route to Highbury for an FA Cup tie in 1927.

Taking centre stage in this photograph is the club's unofficial mascot of the time.

His name is Reg Ellinson and in his self-appointed role he followed Liverpool all over the country in the 1920s.

At every game he would be dressed for the occasion, head-to-toe in red and white, and with his face painted in similar colours. You couldn't miss him.

In his trademark multi-coloured spats, red-draped tailcoat, white trousers that were often muddied due to larking around on the pitch before kick-off, and a red and white top-hat, Reg would stand out in any crowd.

Sometimes he'd carry a prop. Occasionally it would be balloons and other times a walking stick or umbrella. All red and white, of course.

He featured in the local paper a few times and was also once captured on film at Fulham's Craven Cottage in 1926.

Home or away he would orchestrate the crowd before kick-off, like on one of the pictures here where he's standing at the front of the old, uncovered Kop. His various antics and routines would keep everyone amused and entertained, and never more so than on derby day when he would put on an impromptu pre-match show with his young Everton counterpart little Tommy Tucker Tembey.

When the players eventually came out onto the pitch he'd wish them luck, as seen on the photograph with Fred Hopkin, then re-join his mates on the terraces to support the team.

These images prove that mascots at Anfield are nothing new.

LFC'S ORIGINAL MASCOT

The 'Dr Fun' and 'Mighty Red' of his day, Reg Ellinson was born in Liverpool in 1897 and lived in Mossley Hill.

A flamboyant character and natty dresser, he was a natural performer who worked as a Cunard Line entertainer after briefly serving in the First World War.

Sadly, Reg passed away at a relatively young age in 1930 and was an almost forgotten figure until his family rediscovered these photographs.

There was also this cartoon, drawn by his younger brother, that depicts him walking through a crowd of onlookers at Anfield.

Other mascots have since followed in his footsteps at Liverpool, but Reg will always be the original.

CHANGING TIMES...1925-30

35. A SPRINGBOARD FOR THE SPRINGBOKS

A joint team photograph to commemorate the historic Anfield friendly match between Liverpool and a South Africa XI on 1 October 1924.

It was the first time foreign opposition had played in front of the Kop and it turned out to be an occasion of great significance, with two future Reds making a big impression for the visitors.

In what was the ninth of 26 games the touring Springboks played across the UK, Ireland and Holland between August and December that year, the hosts were aiming to become only the second side to defeat them.

But with the Merseyside derby looming at the weekend, the Liverpool team was much-changed from the regular starting eleven and they were in for a rude awakening.

Only David Pratt, Bill Cockburn and Archie Rawlings had played in the previous league game and several reserves players featured. Albert Shears, a forward signed just a month before, scored twice but it was the South Africans who stole the show, running out emphatic 5-2 winners in front of 12,000 onlookers.

The local press was gushing in their praise of the visitors' 'joyous football' and two players in particular caught the eye: goalkeeper Arthur Riley and inside-right Gordon Hodgson.

Two months later, the South Africa team returned to Merseyside to conclude their tour with a 3-2 victory over Everton.

Come the following year, Transvaal duo Riley and Hodgson were back for a third time, this time to sign for Liverpool.

Back row (left to right): *William Findlay, George Brunton, Ernie Brown, George Parry, Ted Parry, Eric Stuart.*
Middle row: *John Wheeler (SA manager), George Patterson (LFC secretary), Bob Tuohy, Bill Cockburn, Friedhelm Scherwin, John Jones, Archie Rawlings, Arthur Riley, Joe Keetley, Matt McQueen (LFC manager).*
Front row: *Alex Skene, Albert Shears, NS Walker, Ephraim Longworth, Charles Thompson, David Pratt, Gordon Hodgson, Hector Lawson, David Murray, Hugh Sweetlove (SA coach).*

36. HODGSON'S CHOICE

The prolific Gordon Hodgson in a familiar pose; unleashing a shot towards the opposition net during his goal-laden decade at Anfield.

In an era when Liverpool often found themselves cast in the shadow of local rivals Everton, inside-forward Hodgson was one of the few shining lights for the Reds.

The Kop's answer to Goodison goalscoring hero Dixie Dean, he was a sharp-shooting South African whose achievements in front of goal set new standards at Anfield.

It didn't take him long to make his mark in a red shirt, serving notice of his potential when scoring two at Old Trafford in only his third game. A first hat-trick quickly followed, and he soon began to make rapid progress up the scoring charts.

In 1930/31 he set a then new club record of 36 league goals in one season, while his eventual tally of 17 Liverpool hat-tricks is yet to be beaten.

Not surprisingly he became a firm favourite among the fans and 'Hodgson's Choice' became a popular shout among the biscuit sellers at Anfield.

A keen all-round sportsman, he also played first-class cricket for Lancashire and excelled at baseball, but it was with a ball at his feet that he achieved legendary status.

His phenomenal goalscoring exploits deserved to reap greater reward in terms of silverware but Hodgson remained remarkably loyal to the club, despite completing 10 years at Anfield without winning a major honour.

He averaged more than 20 goals a season during this time and only Roger Hunt has scored more in the league for Liverpool.

His final total of 241 goals was a record that would stand for over 30 years and, to this day, has only been surpassed twice.

37. BATTLE OF THE MERSEY

Local pride is at stake once again as Liverpool captain Don McKinlay shakes hands with his Everton counterpart Sam Chedgzoy moments before kick-off in the Merseyside derby of February 1926.

Goodison Park was the setting for this meeting of two mid-table teams and on a filthy day weather-wise both sides combined to serve up a treat for the 45,793 spectators who braved the elements.

The action was end-to-end, with six goals shared; the end result a fair one and everyone went home happy.

It was later described as one of the best derby matches seen and McKinlay, having first played in the fixture 14 years earlier, had been involved in more than his fair share.

Regarded as an uncompromising and hard-tackling defender, his legendary status at the club had long been assured.

A double title-winning captain earlier in the decade, the Scot predominantly operated as a left-back but displayed such great versatility that he was equally adept as a wing-half, centre-half and right across the forward line.

Also renowned for packing a fierce shot, the Scot once scored from inside his own half and posed a major threat in dead-ball situations.

A highly consistent performer during the course of his time at Anfield, McKinlay was a true club stalwart who enjoyed one of the longest Liverpool playing careers, joining as an 18-year-old in 1910 and not bowing out until three years after this photograph was taken.

Although born and bred in Glasgow, he made Liverpool his home and in later life worked as a publican, managing, among other pubs, the Greyhound in Knotty Ash.

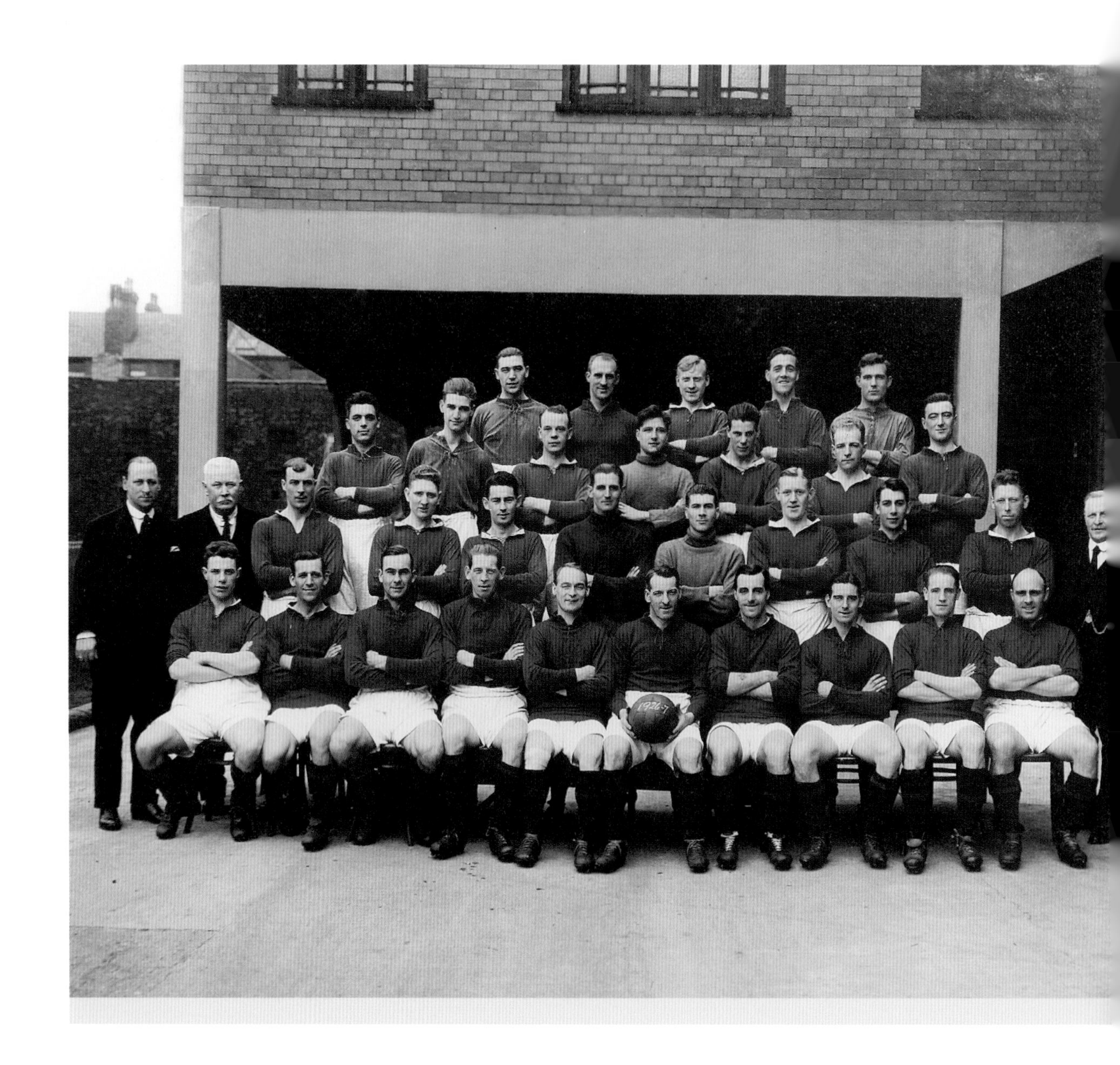
1926-7

38. A TIME OF TRANSITION

A massive squad of players but a season of mid-table mediocrity. This was 1926/27. The glory days of earlier in the decade are starting to fade and the club is entering a major period of transition.

In the car park at the back of the Main Stand a host of familiar faces remain; legends from the title-winning years, memories of their heroic deeds safely stored for eternity.

These players were not getting any younger though and the rebuilding job was underway. At least a couple of future legends are now pictured alongside them, but the process of getting enough adequate replacements onboard was a slow one.

Expectations were higher than ever before, and following in the footsteps of such a talented bunch of players as the Untouchables was proving a tough task.

No surprise then that the strain was beginning to tell, especially on manager Matt McQueen who would soon succumb to the pressure.

This was to be another campaign that did nothing to suggest this team was heading anywhere other than in the wrong direction.

In what was to be his last season as a regular in the first eleven, Harry Chambers would regain his mantle as the club's top marksman, netting 21 times, but it wasn't enough to lift the gloom that was quickly descending over Anfield.

Interest in the FA Cup went no further than the fifth round and for a spell during the first half of the season, Liverpool faced the genuine threat of being sucked into a relegation battle.

That they recovered to finish ninth was ultimately a relief but nothing else and it couldn't paper over the ever-widening cracks that were appearing.

Back row (left to right): *Cyril Oxley, Ephraim Longworth, James Jackson, Tom Bromilow, Fred Baron.* ***Second row:*** *Robert Clark, George Childs, David McMullan, James Trill, Tommy Reid, Danny Shone, Bill Sheppard.* ***Third row:*** *George Patterson (secretary), William Connell (trainer), David Pratt, Tom Scott, Patrick McDade, Arthur Riley, Elisha Scott, William Cockburn, Dick Edmed, Dick Forshaw, Matt McQueen (manager).* ***Front row:*** *Robert Done, Jimmy Gray, Gordon Hodgson, Jock McNab, Tommy Lucas, Don McKinlay, Harry Chambers, Jimmy Walsh, Albert Shears, Fred Hopkin.*

39. GROUNDS FOR OPTIMISM

On and off the pitch there was a renewed, albeit temporary, sense of optimism around the club in 1928/29.

After a worrying few years in which Liverpool's form deteriorated so badly that they only narrowly avoided relegation the previous season, this was to be a campaign that brought some welcome respite to the post-title-winning malaise of the mid-1920s.

The gradual phasing out of the old guard remained a work in progress but new stars started to shine; players like top scorer Gordon Hodgson, Scottish inside-left Jimmy McDougall, winger Dick Edmed and defensive duo Tom Morrison and James Jackson.

The season began with a 3-0 home win against Bury. Irishman Billy Millar scored within a minute of his debut and later grabbed another, while fellow debutant Bert Whitehurst also netted.

That was the first match in which supporters stood under the new Kop roof and Anfield could now boast the largest covered terrace in football. It was capable of housing up to 28,000 and pushed the overall capacity of the ground to beyond 60,000.

The following week Liverpool travelled to Villa Park, where this photograph was taken. McDougall opened the scoring but the home side came back to win 3-1 in what proved to be Don McKinlay's last-ever game for the club.

After hovering around mid-table for much of the season and suffering the almost annual disappointment of exiting the FA Cup before the latter rounds, a late upturn in form saw the Reds finish a creditable fifth in the league table.

It offered hope for a brighter future but unfortunately Liverpool would come nowhere near to scaling these heights for quite a while.

Back row (left to right): *Mr Harvey Webb (director), Fred Hopkin, Albert Whitehurst, Gordon Hodgson, Charlie Wilson (trainer), Elisha Scott, Jimmy McDougall, Billy Millar, Mr Walter Cartwright (director).* ***Front row:*** *David Davidson, Dick Edmed, James Jackson, Don McKinlay, Tommy Morrison, Tom Bromilow.*

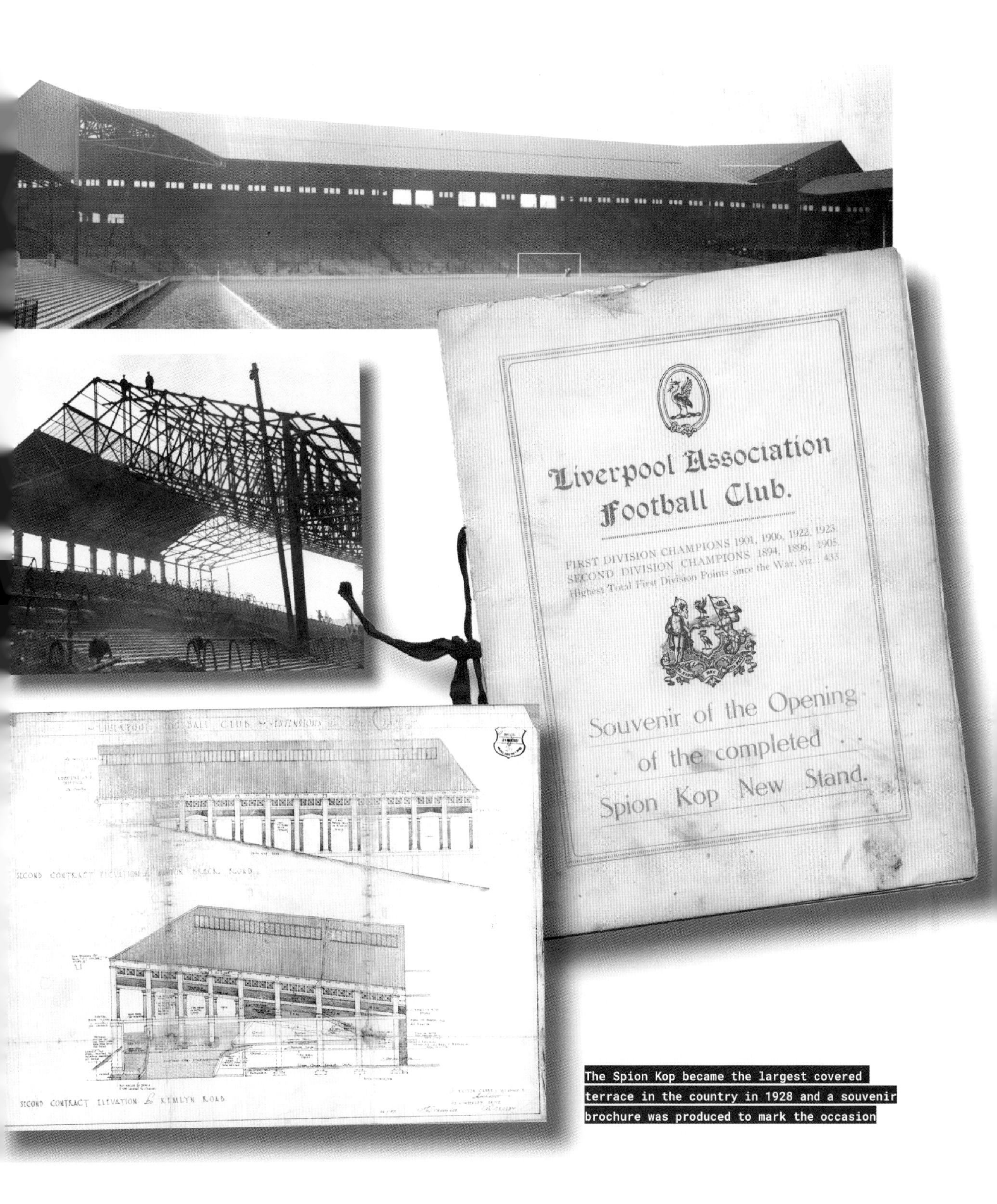

The Spion Kop became the largest covered terrace in the country in 1928 and a souvenir brochure was produced to mark the occasion

Caption on page 104

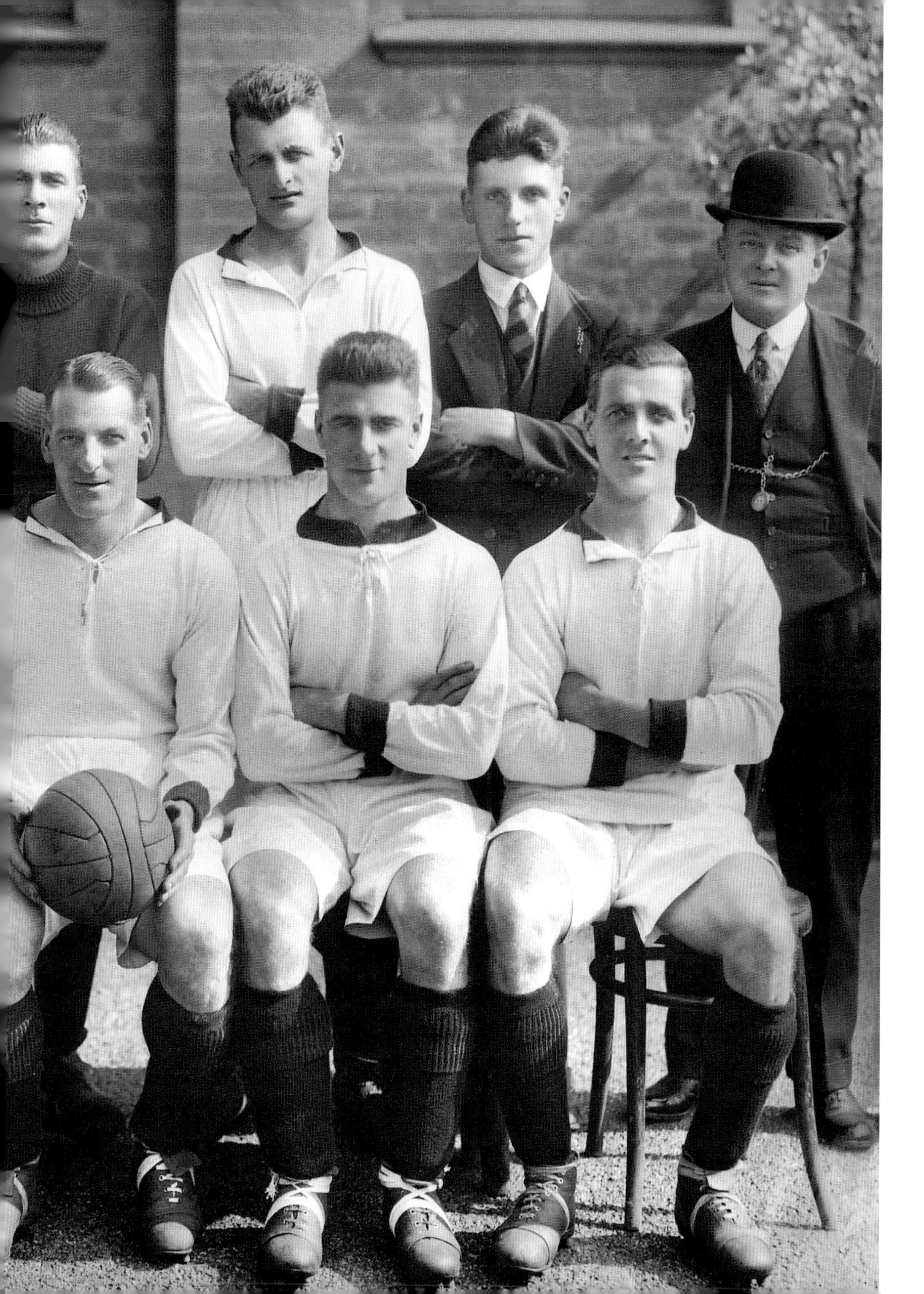

MITCHELLS
BUTLE

40. THE RED REVEREND

Liverpool captain James 'Parson' Jackson challenges Birmingham City forward Joe Bradford during a goalless draw at St Andrew's in March 1929.

A wholehearted and intelligent defender, Jackson proved to be a key asset during an era when the Reds struggled to recapture the success they had enjoyed earlier in the decade.

At his best when playing centre-back, he worked tirelessly and was a natural choice to succeed Tom Bromilow as captain five months before this picture was taken. He skippered for the first time in October 1928, ironically away to Arsenal, the team his father had once captained.

Born in Newcastle and signed from Aberdeen in 1925, Jackson was a devout Christian who studied Greek and Philosophy at Cambridge University.

"I am convinced that my ability to play football is just as much a gift from God as any talent that man possesses," he once said, while a football writer of the time remarked: "If he prays as hard as he plays he ought to be Archbishop of Canterbury in record time!"

Given his church connections, Jackson was famously nicknamed 'Parson' and after hanging up his boots in 1933, he was ordained as a Presbyterian minister and maintained a strong affection for the club, returning in 1947 to officiate at the funeral of chairman WH McConnell.

Left to right: *Harry Race, Tommy Lucas, Jimmy Smith on Gordon Hodgson's shoulders, Jimmy McDougall with Tom Bromilow on his back, Dick Edmed on David Davidson's shoulders, Tom Morrison and Archie McPherson.*

41. TEAMWORK

The Liverpool players are all smiles as they pose for the camera during the build-up to the club's FA Cup third round tie at home to Cardiff City in January 1930.

Pictured at the corner of the now demolished Lake Street, the old Main Stand is visible in the background, to the right.

The Reds were strongly fancied to overcome their Second Division opponents that weekend and optimism was high that it would then be the springboard for a long-awaited lengthy run in the competition.

But, not for the first time when it came to the FA Cup, disappointment lay in store.

Eight of the players seen here went on to play in the following day's game and, before a crowd of 50,141 at Anfield, Archie McPherson opened the scoring, only for their Second Division opponents to hit back with a goal in each half to cause the shock of the round.

Scottish inside-forward McPherson had only joined the club in November. This was his fourth goal in a red shirt but although he remained at the club for a further four years, he would only add another 15 to his tally in that time.

Tom Bromilow is one of the two who didn't feature in the match and his illustrious career with the Reds would soon draw to a close. He moved to Amsterdam at the end of the season to embark on a coaching career that later saw him manage Burnley, Crystal Palace, Newport County and Leicester City.

LIVERPOOL F.C.
TO
F.C. AUSTRIA
LIVERPOOL F.C.
TO

STALLING STARS...1934-39

LIVERPOOL F.C
TO
F.C. AUSTRIA
28TH NOV

42. AUSTRIAN RE-MATCH

Rival captains Thomas 'Tiny' Bradshaw and Walter Nausch exchange pennants ahead of Liverpool's 'Grand Match' with FC Austria at Anfield in November 1934.

This was the second meeting between the two teams in just under a year. The first had gone Liverpool's way but the Austrians made a lasting impression, despite a 4-2 defeat, and enormous interest had been roused in their return.

The visitors prepared with a run through the recently-opened Mersey Tunnel and, boasting a team that contained three members of the famous Austrian 'Wunderteam', including skipper Nausch, they were now considered to be even stronger.

For Liverpool, the not-so-tiny Bradshaw, a club record signing in 1930 and another in a long line of great Scottish centre-halves to have worn the red shirt, was one of six players who had played in the previous year's game.

The Austrians' star attraction was still the prematurely-balding Mattias Sindelaar, scorer of two goals at Anfield in 1933 and widely regarded as one of the best players in the world. He failed to get on the scoresheet this time but once again pulled the strings as the visitors stylishly gained their revenge.

In their vibrant lilac shirts, their 'artistic football' and 'clever manipulation of the ball' had the 16,000 crowd watching on in awe.

Liverpool were not exactly outclassed but two second-half goals condemned them to a 2-0 home defeat in what the local press described as 'a most exciting friendly match'.

43. JOE'S EARLY TASTE OF ANFIELD

Anfield plays host to a prestigious schoolboy game featuring a youngster who, decades later, would go on to achieve immortality with Liverpool.

Positioned third from the right on the back row and fittingly wearing a Liver-Bird-emblazoned red shirt is 14-year-old future club legend Joe Fagan.

He's in the Liverpool schools team that is competing for the WR Williams Memorial Cup, an annual contest played against neighbouring Bootle.

It was always considered one of the highlights of the junior football calendar and this game took place on the evening of Monday 15 April 1935.

A strapping centre-half, young Fagan can be seen towering over the majority of other players and is even taller than the referee.

Although his athletic build lent itself to other sports (he excelled at boxing and cricket too), football remained his first love.

Unusually, he had no particular allegiance to either of the city's two big clubs but growing up on Scotland Road, near the bottom of Everton Valley, the thrill of playing at Anfield would have been huge.

And just as he would be on many times at this venue in years to come, Joe ended up on the winning side.

A few years later, after catching the eye while playing for St Helens-based amateur side Earlestown Bohemians, he was invited back to Anfield for a trial but declined the opportunity to sign.

Instead, Fagan opted to pursue his professional football career with Manchester City. Their gain was Liverpool's loss – but this story was not yet over.

44. WALK ON

A resident peers out from behind the curtains of the corner house to see what all the commotion is about as local school children chase after a group of Liverpool players who have just set off on a brisk stroll along Anfield Road.

It's 1936 and with training walks often part of the club's daily routine, such scenes were commonplace back then.

The 1930s was a decade devoid of silverware but the team remained as revered as ever and autographs would be sought by young supporters at every opportunity.

Of the players pictured, Jimmy McDougall would go on to play more games (356) for the club than the rest, but the ageing Tosh Johnson was the most experienced.

A league and FA Cup winner, with Manchester City and Everton respectively, he had controversially crossed Stanley Park to join Liverpool in 1934.

It's also interesting to note back then that all players were governed by a strict set of rules and regulations, laid out in a tiny red book that was issued to every member of the squad at the start of each season.

In it, they were instructed to report to the ground at 10:15 each morning and again at 2:45 in the afternoon, and also requested to refrain from swearing.

Other stipulations included 'no smoking in the dressing room during training hours', 'no dancing after Wednesday each week' and 'no frequenting clubs where gambling takes place or intoxicants served'.

Hardly the glamorous life.

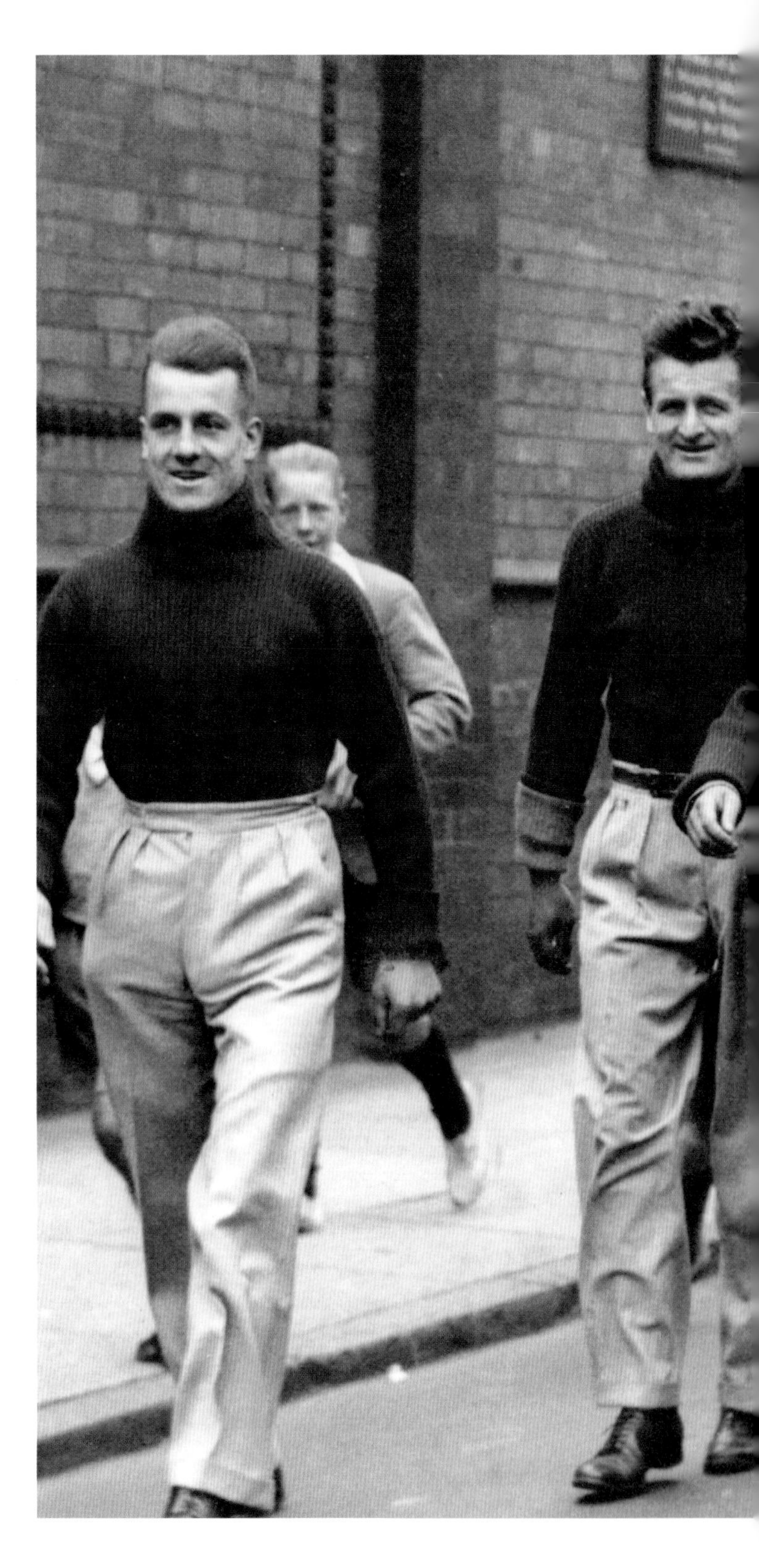

45. SNOOKERED

These Liverpool players of the mid-1930s swap the green grass of Anfield for the green baize of the snooker table as they enjoy some down time in preparation for an upcoming game.

A hushed silence descends over the room as winger Alf Hanson steadies himself in readiness to take his shot.

Among those looking on and waiting for their turn is a youthful-looking future title winner and team manager Phil Taylor. Two other would-be league champions are full-back Jim Harley and inside-forward Harry Eastham.

Fellow youngster John Shafto, along with the more experienced Fred Rogers and Ben Dabbs complete the line-up, but in terms of star status at the time this picture was taken it's Hanson who would have been the main man.

Christened Adolf, but commonly known as Alf, he started out as a junior with Everton before joining Liverpool as an amateur in 1931.

His senior debut for the Reds came two years later and he was a regular in the starting eleven for all but one of the five seasons that followed.

A dashing and highly consistent outside-left, Hanson was renowned for his long-raking stride and thunderous left-footed shots. A constant menace to opposition defenders, he would go on to score an impressive 52 goals in 177 appearances before surprisingly being sold to Chelsea for a then club record £7,500 in 1938.

Left to right: *Phil Taylor, Fred Rogers, Alf Hanson, Jim Harley, John Shafto, Ben Dabbs, Harry Eastham.*

46. 'SETBACK' IN ZAGREB

Reds skipper Ernie Blenkinsop engages in pre-match pleasantries with his opposite number ahead of Liverpool's second game on their 1936 continental tour.

Standing behind Blenkinsop in Zagreb is the club's vice-chairman James Troop, while in the foreground on the left is director George Richards.

After kicking off the trip with a win in Prague, the Reds had rolled into Yugoslavia to play Gradjanski SK, one of the country's most popular and successful teams during the inter-war years.

For the hosts this was a game of major significance. Although a dominant force domestically, they were a club who measured success on how they fared internationally and an excited crowd of 20,000 were in attendance for the visit of Liverpool.

In his role as captain, full-back Blenkinsop, a former England international who had been signed from Sheffield Wednesday in 1934, would regularly update *Echo* readers with his thoughts from the tour and when commenting on this particular game he described it as 'a real setback'.

Despite a goal from Berry Nieuwenhuys, the hosts romped to a resounding 5-1 victory.

Blenkinsop went on to describe Liverpool's performance as 'a very poor affair' but in their defence raised question marks about the state of the pitch and the dubious standard of refereeing.

Obviously stung by this defeat, a rematch on home soil was immediately sought and six months later Liverpool returned the compliment by welcoming the Yugoslavs to Anfield and handing out a 4-1 beating.

Left to right: *Matt Busby, Berry 'Nivvy' Niewenhuys, Ernie Blenkinsop (captain), Phil Taylor, Tom 'Tiny' Bradshaw, Tom Bush, Alf Hobson, Alf Hanson, Syd Roberts, Fred Howe, Ben Dabbs.*

47. FLYING THE FLAG

The Liverpool players take to the field in Belgrade ahead of their third game on the 1936 post-season tour.

In recognition of their visit, a Union Jack flag flies from the top of the stand behind them and the team shows two changes from the one that had lost in Zagreb four days earlier.

On this occasion a much-improved performance saw the Reds get back to winning ways against Beogradski (later renamed OFK Belgrade).

A goal apiece from Bootle-born duo Alf Hanson and Syd Roberts sent them racing into a 2-0 lead and that's how it stayed.

The English visitors had been warmly welcomed in Yugoslavia, with the red carpet rolled out for them at every opportunity. Photographs of several Liverpool players even appeared in the window displays of some local shops, such was the excitement generated by the club's first-ever trip to this part of Europe.

The travelling party were enjoying it so much that they extended their stay and added another fixture to the schedule.

It was against the same opponents, at the same venue, three days later. Hanson scored again, so too did Berry Nieuwenhuys, but this time it was the hosts that ran out 3-2 winners.

After Belgrade, Liverpool moved on to complete their tour with the final two games being played in Romania, both of which were won, meaning when they finally returned home after almost a month on the road, they did so with four victories from six.

The club's travelling party in Belgrade

48. BARE-CHESTED IN BELGRADE

Some confusion surrounds the story behind these three images.

They are of the Liverpool team in Belgrade during the tour in 1936, that is for sure.

But because they are dated 24 May, which, as records show, is the day of their second game in the Yugoslav capital, it has often been reported that the pictures are from the actual match and that, due to a clash of colours, Liverpool played with no tops on.

There is, however, no firm evidence to substantiate this claim.

In his regular tour updates, published by the *Echo*, Ernie Blenkinsop made no reference to playing bare-chested and also commented that the game was played in 'six inches of deep clay', which doesn't look to be the case here.

A more reasonable explanation is that these photographs were actually taken before, during and after a training session, possibly on one of the days in between the two games in Belgrade.

The team picture, including trainer Charlie Wilson, a member of the club's first-ever title winning side, shows all the players who travelled to the Balkans apart from Tom Bush.

In the action image, with the Serbian countryside providing a scenic background, Wilson can be seen watching over a practice match between the Liverpool players, who are then captured sitting around the table having a well-earned drink.

Back row (left to right): *Charlie Wilson (trainer), Matt Busby, Ben Dabbs, Berry Nieuwenhuys, Ted Savage, Alf Hobson, Syd Roberts, Norman Low, Tiny Bradshaw.* ***Front row:*** *Harry Eastham, Ernie Blenkinsop, Fred Howe, Alf Hanson, Phil Taylor.*

49. SPECIAL KAY

New Liverpool manager George Kay receives a warm welcome on his first day at Anfield in August 1936.

Captain Ernie Blenkinsop shakes hands with the 44-year-old incoming boss while the rest of the team, coaching staff and some directors look on.

Kay's appointment signalled the start of a new era at the club with the dual role of secretary-manager now a thing of the past. While previous incumbent George Patterson reverted to secretarial duties, Kay's remit was solely to manage the team.

Recruited from Southampton on a salary of £600, he was born in Manchester and, as a player, captained West Ham in the first-ever Wembley FA Cup final. His management career began at Luton before a five-year stint in charge of the Second Division Saints.

Although he'd not managed in the top-flight, Kay was highly-respected within the game and beat off competition from 51 other applicants, including Anfield legend Tom Bromilow, to land the job.

Renowned for his deep thinking and innovative ideas, he was described as a man of 'great energy', while shrewd tactical nous and good man-management skills were also listed among his many attributes.

The task ahead of him though was a tough one. He took control of a team that had been in serious decline for too long and one that had only narrowly avoided relegation the previous season.

'One of the most important appointments to one of the most important posts', was how the *Echo* reported the news of his arrival and Kay would gradually transform the team's fortunes – but success was far from instant.

Alf Hanson (right) and Berry Nieuwenhuys (below right) are two of the stars of the 1937-38 Liverpool team whose signatures appear below

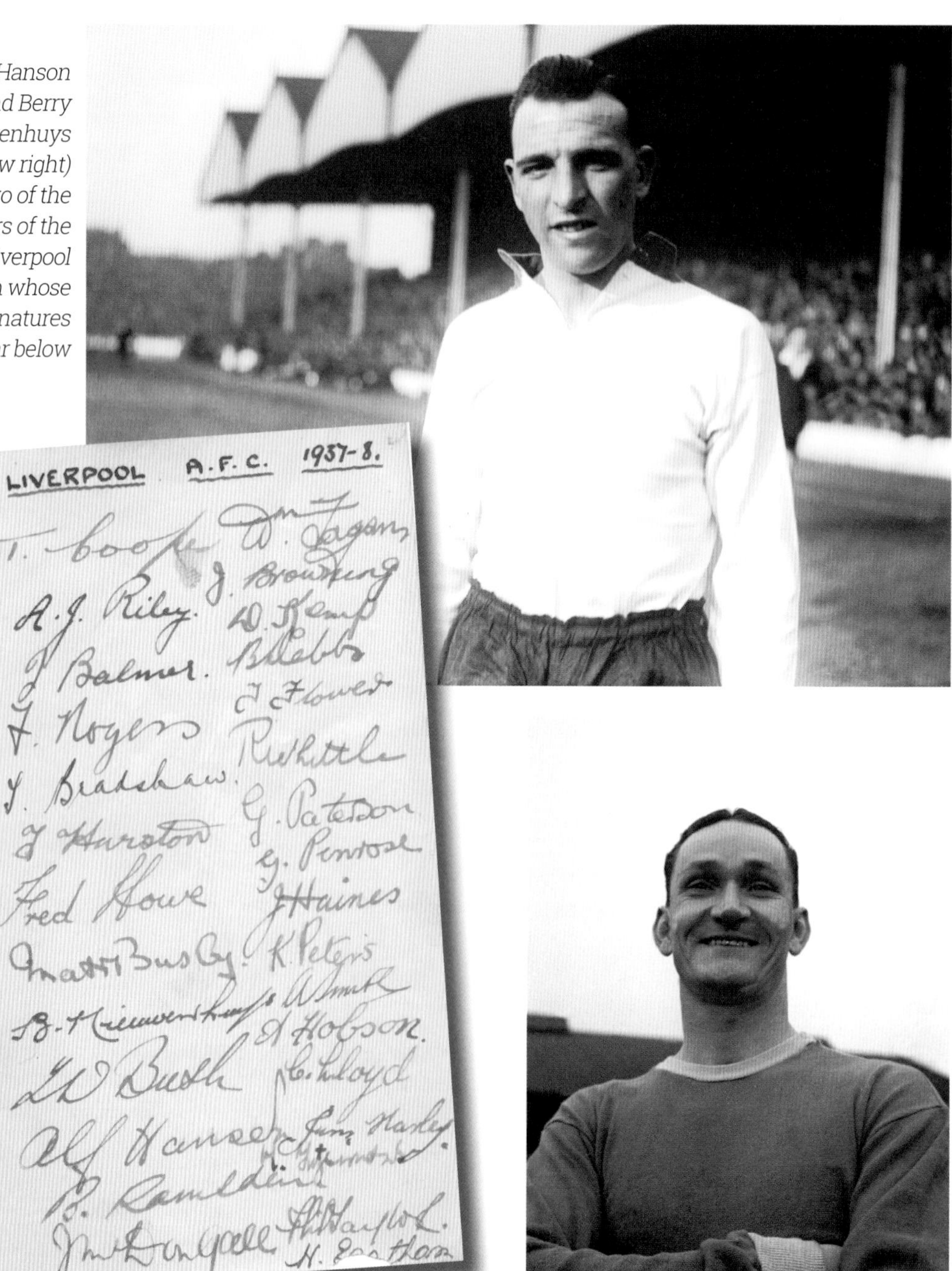

50. NEW SEASON, NEW HOPE

It's the summer of 1937 and the Liverpool squad report back to Anfield for the start of pre-season training.

The season before had been one to forget – an 18th-place finish in the league and a third-round FA Cup exit to Norwich – but a fresh start brought with it the usual bouts of optimism.

And even though the new campaign was to get off to an inauspicious start, with a 1-6 hammering at Stamford Bridge, things would get better.

In his second year as manager, George Kay was starting to make his presence felt and a much-improved Liverpool moved seven places up the table and progressed to the fifth round of the FA Cup.

Highlights of the season included a 3-1 win at Goodison in which Jack Balmer scored after just 10 seconds.

South African outside-right Berry Nieuwenhuys, more commonly known as 'Nivvy', made most appearances, while Alf Hanson topped the scoring charts with 15 goals in what was to be his last season as a Liverpool player.

51. 'SNOWY' IN DEMAND

With their autograph books at the ready, a group of young Liverpudlians eagerly seize the opportunity to collect a new signature after spotting one of their heroes in the Anfield car park.

While manager George Kay, cigarette hanging from his lips, waits patiently in the wings, his star full-back and captain Tom Cooper responds diligently to the many requests that come his way.

Always a big favourite with the fans, Cooper was an influential figure in the Liverpool team of the 1930s.

A former England international, who had also captained his country, his arrival from Derby County in December 1934 was considered a major coup.

It cost the club a then record outlay of £7,500 to secure his services but it was a fee that he more than justified. Although 29 at the time, the experienced Cooper still had plenty to offer and was a regular in the years that followed.

Affectionately known as 'Snowy', due to the fairness of his hair, he was a stylish right-back who skippered the side between 1936 and 1939.

Like so many talented Liverpool players of this generation, his time at Anfield unfortunately coincided with a major barren spell in terms of silverware.

Nevertheless, Cooper's Liverpool career was a highly-distinguished one.

Described as 'one of the finest full-backs English football has known and one of the nicest of men', he served the Reds admirably, never scoring a goal but clocking up 160 appearances.

Back row: *Jimmy McInnes, Phil Taylor, Jim Harley, Dirk Kemp, Tom Bush, Barney Ramsden, Tom Cooper.*
Front row: *Berry Nieuwenhuys, Willie Fagan, Matt Busby, Jack Balmer, Harman Van Den Berg.*

52. READY FOR BATTLE

Proud captain Matt Busby takes centre stage ahead of what would be the shortest season on record.

On the eve of the 1939/40 campaign this Liverpool team appeared to have not a care in the world but with war clouds looming ominously, football's importance was fast diminishing.

Little did they know when this photograph was taken that their careers would soon be put on hold.

After just three First Division fixtures, war was officially declared, the season immediately curtailed, and all results expunged from the record books.

For teenage centre-forward Cyril Done (pictured inset) this was a particular shame because he had scored on his debut in the previous game. On the flip side, Jim Harley had been sent off but never served his suspension. Both players would still have a key role in the future, as did Phil Taylor, Jack Balmer, Berry Nieuwenhuys and Willie Fagan, even though war would rob them of their best years. Barney Ramsden and Tom Bush both played a part in the title-winning team of '47, with the latter going on to join the coaching staff.

The rest never played competitively for the club again. Dirk Kemp and Harman Van Den Berg eventually returned to South Africa. Jimmy McInnes took up a position behind the scenes at Anfield, while Matt Busby turned down a similar offer and went from being pre-war Liverpool skipper to post-war manager of Manchester United.

The most tragic case though was that of Cooper who, less than a year after this photo had been taken, was sadly killed in a motorcycle accident.

Left to right: *Matt Busby, Jack Balmer, Jim Harley, Willie Fagan, Dirk Kemp.*

53. CALL OF DUTY

Five members of the Liverpool first-team squad pack their bags, don their uniforms, and bid Anfield a fond farewell as they set off to serve their country in the Second World War.

For Matt Busby, Jack Balmer, Jim Harley, Willie Fagan and Dirk Kemp, not to mention the rest of their team-mates who aren't pictured, life was about to change irrevocably. The future was shrouded in uncertainty.

Prior to the onset of hostilities, Liverpool had been the first team in Britain to register all their players – plus manager George Kay and assistant secretary Jack Rouse – with the Territorial Army.

In total, during the course of the six-year conflict, 76 players from Liverpool would experience active service, a figure bettered by only two other clubs, Wolves and Crystal Palace.

Football did continue to be played throughout the war and it was in these wartime regional leagues and supplementary cup competitions that many promising youngsters pulled on a red shirt for the first time, notably future greats Billy Liddell and Bob Paisley, who had been signed on as youngsters in the immediate pre-war years.

Several high-profile players from other clubs guested for Liverpool too, among them Stan Cullis and Dennis Westcott of Wolves, Manchester City goalkeeper Frank Swift, Charlton duo Sam Bartram and Don Welsh, and, from Preston North End, a certain Bill Shankly.

Fortunes, not surprisingly varied throughout this time but Liverpool did enjoy some success when winning the Football League North in 1943. They also collected a couple of Liverpool Senior Cups and the Lancashire Senior Cup.

BACK WITH A BANG...1946-47

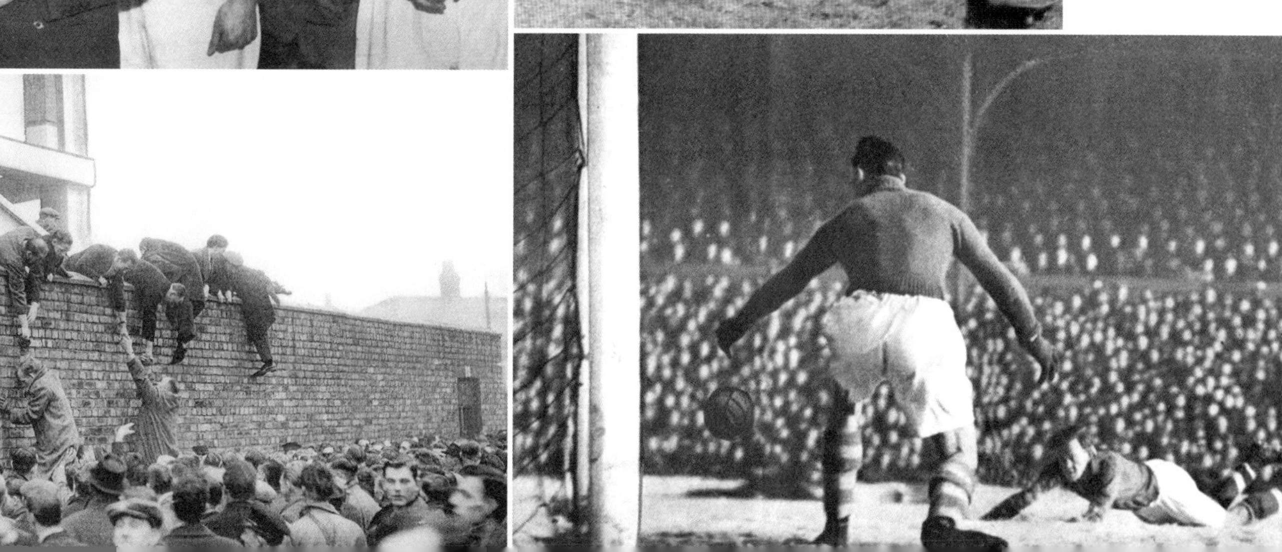

54. BRAWN IN THE USA

Pioneering Liverpool chairman Bill McConnell stands proudly alongside the team at Randall's Island in New York during the club's historic post-war tour of North America.

McConnell was the brains behind this ground-breaking trip that would prepare the Reds for their long-awaited return to 'proper football' in 1946/47.

A caterer who ran a string of dockside cafes, he was a firm believer in the nutritional benefits that could be reaped by escaping the bleak austerity of food-rationed Britain.

And so, it was on a diet of giant t-bone steaks, eggs, vegetables and freshly squeezed orange juice that the players lavishly dined out on for the duration of their stay stateside.

It was the first time a Liverpool team had ever crossed the Atlantic and it proved to be an inspired decision by McConnell, who would sadly pass away just over a year after this tour.

Of course, they played some football too – ten matches in eight different cities, all in the space of four weeks. They won every one, most of them convincingly, and were feted wherever they went.

The trip had been such a success that the club was invited to stay on and play further games against teams from Mexico and possibly Costa Rica, but with the start of the new Football League season looming, it was an offer that had to be politely declined.

This photograph was taken at the Triborough Stadium ahead of the third game. It was against a team comprising of the best players the American League had to offer but, like all the others, they were no match for 'England's Star Booters', as Liverpool were often referred to in the American press.

For the second consecutive game Cyril Done scored a hat-trick, with Jack Balmer and Bob Priday also netting in a 5-0 win.

"I think we rather surprised the soccerites of USA by our superiority," reflected manager George Kay when the tour eventually concluded and there would soon be plenty more surprises in store for their opponents back home.

The players had gained in confidence and strength, all of which would stand them in good stead for the momentous season which lay ahead.

Back row (left to right): *Jim Harley, Barney Ramsden, Willie Fagan, Tom Bush, Bill McConnell (chairman), Jack Balmer, Cyril Sidlow, Eddie Spicer, Kenneth Seddon, Harry Eastham, Albert Shelley.*
Front row: *Cyril Done, Bob Priday, Phil Taylor, Laurie Hughes, Bob Paisley, Berry Nieuwenhuys.*

55. FANS FLOCK BACK

Football in England was never more popular than in the immediate post-war period. Supporters who had been starved of their regular footy-fix during the hostilities flocked back to grounds in record numbers.

Anfield experienced this attendance boom as much as anywhere else and the scenes captured here, on Boxing Day 1946, are typical of the time.

Stoke City, with star attraction Stanley Matthews among their ranks, were the visitors to L4 and with both clubs battling it out at the top of the table, interest was even higher.

As fans spilled out of the local pubs after enjoying a few festive pre-match pints, this was the sight that greeted them. The Kop turnstiles were closed shortly before kick-off and 20,000 were reportedly locked outside.

Those lucky enough to be inside witnessed a 2-0 victory for the Reds, with Berry Nieuwenhuys and Albert Stubbins netting the goals that avenged a 2-1 defeat in the corresponding fixture at the Victoria Ground 24 hours earlier.

Come the end of the season the importance of this result would become much clearer.

As for the crowd, the official attendance of 49,465 was by no means the biggest recorded at Anfield that season. It was, in fact, topped on 10 occasions but the season average of 45,917 set a new club record.

56. ICE-COOL ALBERT'S SNOW STUNNER

Albert Stubbins does his best Superman impression to get his head on the end of a Billy Liddell cross and score one of the greatest goals ever seen at Anfield.

It came in the FA Cup quarter-final at home to Birmingham City on 1 March 1947, the second of three he famously scored that day, but the one for which he will forever be most remembered by Liverpudlians.

Signed for a club record fee from Newcastle United earlier in the season, the ginger-haired Geordie had hit the ground running in a red shirt and was already on his way to achieving cult-status among the fans.

His goals had not only helped fire Liverpool into contention for the title, they also raised hopes of a first FA Cup final appearance in 33 years.

With cup fever sweeping through the red half of the city, interest in this tie was almost unprecedented and this was the first all-ticket game in Anfield history.

Blizzards during the week had left the pitch covered in a blanket of snow but Liverpool adapted best and took a first-half lead through Stubbins. Birmingham equalised with a penalty before Jack Balmer restored the Reds' advantage.

Then came the moment of the match, the now legendary 'goal in the snow'.

From a free-kick on the left, Liddell swung a low ball into the penalty area. There looked to be no real danger until Stubbins, lurking near the far post, flung himself horizontally through the air just inches off the ground.

He connected with his head and the ball flew past 'keeper Gil Merrick like a rocket. Although the momentum of the dive sent him skidding across the ice and he cut his knees, it was a small price to pay for a place in Anfield folklore.

Sixteen minutes later Stubbins completed his hat-trick to confirm Liverpool's passage into the last four for the first time in over three decades. It had been an unforgettable afternoon.

57. THE ORIGINAL CRAZY GANG

A team on the cusp of greatness, this is the Liverpool class of 1946/47 ahead of what would be a pivotal few weeks for them.

Their best years may have been lost to the war but as the run-in to the inaugural post-war season loomed, these men now carried on their shoulders the hopes of every Liverpudlian.

This so-called 'Crazy Gang', a moniker bequeathed on them long before it became associated with the Wombles from Plough Lane in the 1980s, had unexpectedly mounted a serious challenge for honours.

As spring approached, they found themselves among the chasing pack near the top of the First Division and just one step away from a place in the FA Cup final.

Given the club's lack of success in the knockout competition, the main focus was on potential success in the latter – especially with a semi-final tie against Second Division Burnley to come.

This photograph was commissioned to celebrate Liverpool reaching the last four and was captured just a week after the quarter-final victory, prior to a league game against Blackburn Rovers. Indeed, so soon after the cup match was this picture taken, Albert Stubbins was still suffering the scars from his famous 'goal in the snow' and had a bandage on his knee, as did Jack Balmer.

Unfortunately, dreams of a first-ever FA Cup triumph were to be cruelly shattered by a semi-final replay defeat against their previous nemesis in claret and blue.

It would have been no consolation at the time but Liverpool were free to concentrate on the league, even if they were considered rank outsiders in a fascinating title race.

Back row (left to right): *George Kay (manager), Jim Harley, Phil Taylor, Ray Lambert, Cyril Sidlow, Bob Paisley, Bill Jones, Billy Liddell, Albert Shelley (trainer).* **Front row:** *Willie Fagan, Jack Balmer, Bill McConnell (chairman), Albert Stubbins, Cyril Done.*

58. HIGH STAKES AT MOLINEUX

Molineux, 31 May 1947. Opposing captains Jack Balmer and Stan Cullis shake hands as Liverpool and Wolves prepare to contest their 42nd and final league game of what was then the longest season on record.

Exactly nine months since the inaugural post-war campaign kicked off, the destiny of the First Division championship had boiled down to the outcome of just two games and for both teams here, the stakes could hardly have been higher.

Long-time league leaders Wolves needed one more win to be crowned champions. A win or draw for Liverpool though would keep them in the hunt and take it to the wire, while also handing a lifeline to Stoke City, who weren't scheduled to complete their season for another two weeks.

The authorities, however, were so confident of a victory for the team in old gold shirts that they had arranged for the trophy to be at the ground, ready and waiting for the anticipated post-match presentation to the retiring Cullis.

That script hadn't been posted to Anfield though and the Crazy Gang lived up to their name by proceeding to gate-crash the expected party.

On a baking hot day in the Black Country, Wolves' title hopes wilted as goals from Balmer and Albert Stubbins, the club's joint-top scorers that season, fired the visitors into a shock first-half lead.

Although the hosts managed to reduce the deficit, Cyril Sidlow's goalkeeping heroics ensured they held on amid intense pressure to claim a priceless victory.

They now faced a nervous two-week wait to see if it would be enough to keep them at the top.

59. A TRIUMPH AGAINST ADVERSITY

Against all odds Liverpool did it and after a tumultuous, unforgettable and, at times, seemingly never-ending season, the time had finally come for the 1946/47 Football League champions to be officially crowned.

There's no pomp, no glitz, no fuss. This is just how it was back then, and these players probably wouldn't have wanted it any other way.

The first post-war campaign finished so late that the trophy presentation had to wait until the start of the next season, and even then, it took place behind closed doors.

In the sanctuary of the Anfield boardroom, with just a handful of officials watching on, the debonair-looking Reds captain Willie Fagan steps up, on behalf of the club, to receive the prize, while team-mates Albert Stubbins and Billy Liddell, two of the key players in this most remarkable of triumphs, collect their medals but look like they can't wait to get back out onto the pitch.

It was a moment of deserved recognition for the endeavours of a team that constantly defied the doubters during a season in which almost everything had been thrown at them.

Amid continued rationing and enforced power cuts, the ongoing threat of a players' strike and the most adverse of weather conditions, a heart-breaking FA Cup exit and an unprecedented fixture pile-up, the Crazy Gang refused to be written off.

When the dust finally settled and Stoke had failed to win their last game, it was Liverpool who were left sitting proud at the top of the First Division table and no-one could deny them this glorious achievement.

Following the long, barren, trophy-less years of the pre-war era, the good times were back.

VANS SPARSHATTS

A TIME OF HEROES...1949-55

60. HIGHBURY HIGH

Against the backdrop of Highbury's famous North Bank terrace, the Liverpool team are pictured prior to a 2-1 victory over Arsenal on 3 September 1949.

With manager George Kay looking every inch a mafia don, this was a side that oozed confidence.

In what was their fifth fixture of the campaign, Albert Stubbins netted twice to maintain an unbeaten start that would stretch to 19 games, setting what was then a new club record. It was a mark that would not be bettered until 1988.

Apart from the introduction of Jimmy Payne and Kevin Baron, this was virtually the same team that had been crowned champions three seasons earlier and it could be argued that this was an even better side.

It wasn't until December that Liverpool's class of 1949/50 suffered their first loss and they remained in contention for a coveted league and FA Cup double right up until the closing weeks of the season.

Unfortunately, a late dip in form put paid to hopes of a second title in four years while all but one of the eleven players that faced Arsenal here, lined up against them in the FA Cup final at Wembley seven months later.

***Back row (left to right):** Phil Taylor, Eddie Spicer, Laurie Hughes, Cyril Sidlow, Ray Lambert, Bob Paisley, George Kay (manager).*
***Front row:** Jimmy Payne, Kevin Baron, Albert Stubbins, Willie Fagan, Billy Liddell.*

61. ON OUR WAY TO WEMBLEY

The 1950 FA Cup final is just days away and excitement is reaching fever pitch as the Liverpool team prepares to leave Lime Street for their pre-Wembley base.

With hundreds of well-wishers lining the platform, Ray Lambert responds to some last-minute autograph requests while fellow Welshman Cyril Sidlow settles into his seat for the journey south.

Liverpool's historic first visit to Wembley is the only topic of conversation in the city the players are escaping. It's the club's second appearance in the final and everyone is praying that the disappointment of defeat in 1914 will not be repeated.

The team's run to this final had been an impressive one. Blackburn, Exeter, Stockport, Blackpool and then neighbours Everton, in the semi-final at Maine Road, had all been beaten, with Lambert and Sidlow featuring in every game.

Full-back Lambert had been a Liverpool player since he was 13, while Sidlow joined from Wolves in 1946. Both were part of the First Division title-winning team of 1946/47 and were now hoping to complete the set.

For all the Liverpool team, the biggest game of their careers was now just two days away and, laden with good luck messages, they headed to their Weybridge 'retreat' in confident mood.

Arsenal lay in wait at Wembley and no matter what the result, it was going to be a momentous occasion.

Royal appointment: *Laurie Hughes shakes hands with King George VI as captain Phil Taylor introduces the Liverpool team prior to the 1950 FA Cup final. Also pictured are Eddie Spicer, Kevin Baron and Bill Jones.*

62. NO CUP LUCK

On what was Liverpool's first-ever appearance at Wembley, inside-forward Kevin Baron shoots towards goal in front of 100,000 supporters during the 1950 FA Cup final against Arsenal.

This was the day everyone at the club had been striving for since 1914 and hopes were high that the most coveted trophy in football back then could finally be brought back to Anfield.

Due to the obvious colour clash both sides changed from their usual red, with Arsenal sporting gold shirts while Liverpool donned their traditional away strip, but with unusual blue and white hooped socks.

The omission of Bob Paisley from the team, despite him having scored in the semi-final, was the big talking point beforehand, while Baron, who had not yet turned 24, was the youngest member of Liverpool's cup final team.

In what was his breakthrough season as a first-team player, he had figured in all the games en route to Wembley and, while not renowned as a prolific goalscorer, scored in the fourth-round victory over Exeter.

Unfortunately, he didn't get many chances to repeat the feat beneath the twin towers and this was a rare opportunity that fell to him.

The scoreboard shows Liverpool were trailing 1-0, to an 18th-minute Reg Lewis goal, and with half-time approaching, Arsenal captain Joe Mercer, pictured on the right, managed to block this effort.

Try as they might, Liverpool were unable to breach the Gunners rearguard and when Lewis scored again just after the hour mark there was no way back.

Baron continued at Liverpool for a further four years but would never get close to playing in a game of this magnitude again.

He passed away in 1971, aged just 45, and another sad footnote to his story is that in 1989 his elder brother Gerard Baron was the oldest victim of the Hillsborough disaster.

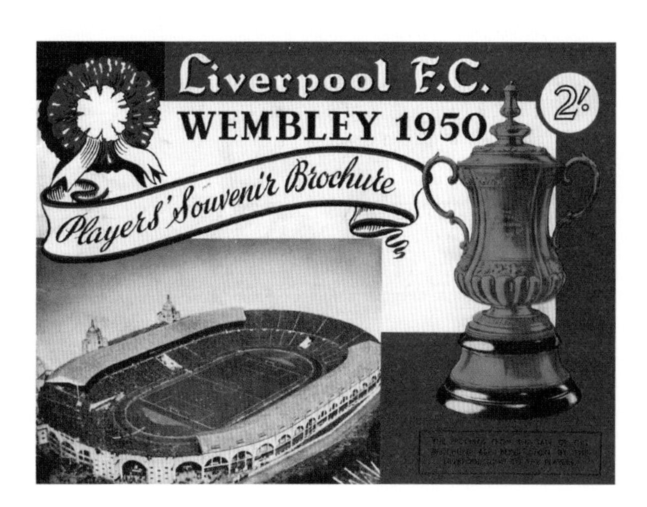

NATIONAL SAVINGS
ARSENAL 1 LIVERPOOL 0

63. LFC LOYALISTS

They captained, coached and managed the team, and are two of the finest servants the club has ever known. Professional to the core and unwaveringly loyal, this is Phil Taylor and Bob Paisley at the peak of their playing careers.

In that classic Liverpool away strip of the time, they are first out of the tunnel at Old Trafford for a Division One fixture in 1950.

Taylor, the elder of the pair by two years, had been signed from his hometown club, Bristol Rovers, in 1936. A clever and elegant wing-half, he took over the captaincy in 1949.

Paisley, a tough and tenacious half-back, hailed from the north-east and joined the Reds from Bishop Auckland the year war was declared.

Their playing styles may have been polar opposites, but they established a strong friendship, and their careers became entwined.

Together they were title winners in 1946/47 and helped steer Liverpool to the FA Cup final in 1950. But, while Taylor became the first man to lead the team out at Wembley, Paisley suffered the bitter disappointment of not being selected on that big day.

This almost led to him turning his back on football altogether but thankfully he was talked around. As the club's fortunes dipped, Paisley occasionally stepped up as stand-in skipper when Taylor was unavailable, and their playing contracts were to expire on the same day in 1954.

Both were offered roles on the backroom staff and eventually worked their way up to the top job. For Taylor that chance would come a lot sooner, but that's where the similarities ended and his long association with the club came to an end in 1959, while Paisley remained for a further 24 years.

64. SILENCING THE POMPEY CHIMES

Jimmy Payne ghosts in at the far post to score the opening goal of a 3-1 win at Fratton Park in December 1950.

It was the first of two goals Payne netted this day and it came via an in-swinging Billy Liddell corner in the 31st minute.

He went on to double Liverpool's advantage in the second half, and although reigning champions Portsmouth pulled a goal back, Jack Balmer completed the scoring seven minutes from time.

A boyhood Evertonian, Bootle-born Payne had been on Liverpool's books since 1942, turning professional two years later but not making his senior debut until 1948.

A small but tricky outside-right, his playing style drew comparisons with that of the famous England international Stanley Matthews and he was therefore duly dubbed the 'Merseyside Matthews'.

Although a regular in the line-up, he wasn't renowned for his prowess in front of goal, scoring just 43 in 243 games during the course of almost eight years in the Liverpool first team, so for him to register twice in a game like this was a rarity.

In April 1956 he was surprisingly sold to neighbours Everton but injuries restricted his appearances for the Blues and he retired to become a newsagent soon after.

SPARSHATTS

65. SICK AS A CANARY

There was FA Cup frustration at Carrow Road in 1951 as Liverpool fell victim to a major giant-killing.

After going all the way to Wembley the previous year, it was hoped that experience would spur them on to go one better this time around.

The third-round draw had been kind, but this trip to Norwich turned into a nightmare.

The Canaries, managed by ex-Red Norman Low, were flying high at the top of Division Three South and had not lost for 22 games.

Liverpool remained huge favourites but the omens were not good. The last time they had failed to clear the first hurdle of the competition was in 1937, when they succumbed at the same venue.

Boosted by the return of Albert Stubbins following a five-week absence, the Reds were able to field eight of the players beaten in the final by Arsenal and should have had nothing to fear.

Pictured here are Stubbins, John Heydon and Jimmy Payne (sliding in) during a Liverpool attack but it was a rare opportunity and one that petered out.

When the minnows eventually broke the deadlock through Tom Docherty just after the hour mark, it came as no surprise.

Noel Kinsey added a second before Docherty scored again and with just ten minutes then remaining Liverpool's fate was all but sealed.

By the time Jack Balmer netted a consolation it was too little too late.

After going so close to cup glory a year before, Liverpool, it seemed, had reverted to type in the world's greatest domestic knockout competition.

Toffee de Luxe

Left to right (seated): *Councillor Will Harrop, Mr James Troop, Mr Harvey Webb, Mr George Richards (chairman), Mr Ralph Milne, Mr Lawson Martindale, Mr Thomas Valentine Williams.* ***(Standing):*** *Alderman Stanley Ronald Williams, Mr Tom McConnell.*

66. WHO'S THE BOSS?

The Liverpool directors convene for a special meeting at the Adelphi Hotel on 15 February 1951. Top of the agenda is to assess the long list of applicants for the newly-vacant managerial position.

It follows the previous month's resignation of George Kay due to ill-health.

Kay's sudden departure had left the team without a manager but there had been no shortage of interest in what was still perceived as one of the most coveted jobs in football.

The task now was to 'cut the wheat from the chaff' and shortlist the leading candidates. Among them was former Anfield favourite Gordon Hodgson, now managing Leeds United, and a young Bill Shankly, who was just starting out in management with Carlisle United.

Shankly was interviewed but his bullish

insistence that he picked the team did not do him any favours with the directors at the time who were reluctant to hand over total control of all team affairs.

Several board members were big admirers of the job 40-year-old Don Welsh was doing with Brighton & Hove Albion in the Third Division South.

Welsh had been a popular guest player at Anfield during the war and was considered for a coaching role at the club in 1945 but opted to continue his playing career instead.

Although he never directly applied for the post, he was sounded out and agreed to a chat.

On 5 March, Welsh, a Mancunian like his predecessor Kay, was announced as Liverpool's new manager and officially took charge 16 days later.

67. CROWDED HOUSE

Former head groundsman Bert Riley chats to female supporters in the Paddock as a record crowd packs into Anfield to see Liverpool play Wolverhampton Wanderers in February 1952.

Cup tie rattles and rosettes are out in force and a place in the fifth round of the FA Cup is at stake as excitement builds prior to kick-off.

Wolves were one of the leading teams of the time and demand for stand tickets had been so great that an editorial in the matchday programme revealed they could have been sold eight times over.

On what was to be a memorable afternoon, long queues had started forming hours before. The gates were closed early and as the players came out, supporters on the Kop were spilling onto the cinder track.

For only the third time in Anfield history, the attendance would top the 60,000-mark and the official figure of 61,905 was 869 more than the previous best, set in 1934, also for an FA Cup tie, against Tranmere Rovers.

As for the actual match, an inspired tactical switch by Don Welsh, that saw Billy Liddell and Cyril Done swap positions, left the visitors bemused and paved the way for a famous Liverpool victory, with Bob Paisley and Done scoring inside the first nine minutes.

Although the Reds' cup run came to an end at Burnley in the next round, it's a day that's long been remembered and until the Anfield capacity is sufficiently increased, that attendance record remains safe.

Another record from back then belonged to the recently-retired Riley. He had been working at Anfield since 1908 and was once the club's longest-serving employee. His son Arthur succeeded him as head groundsman and the family's association with the club would eventually span almost three quarters of a century.

68. SEASIDE SPECIAL

Manager Don Welsh (far right) puts the players through an unusual training routine on Blackpool seafront in January 1955 as preparations are stepped up ahead of a forthcoming FA Cup tie against Mersey rivals Everton.

A quirky character, who was renowned for such eccentricities as doing handstands in the dressing room, Welsh's coaching style could be slightly unconventional at times.

Taking the team away to a seaside resort ahead of big games was nothing new but he often favoured more innovative and engaging methods to maintain the players' fitness.

Instead of relentless running around a track, recreational keep-fit games, such as leap-frog and tunnel-ball, plus exercises like we see here were introduced.

A few days later the Reds pulled off arguably the most surprising result in Merseyside derby history to book their place in the fifth round of the FA Cup.

It was a tie that had the whole city buzzing with anticipation. First Division Everton against Second Division Liverpool at Goodison Park and 72,000 were in attendance to witness the expected slaughter of Welsh's team.

The manager got his tactics right, though, and a plan to exploit the hosts' offside trap worked to perfection. Billy Liddell and Alan A'Court fired Liverpool into a 2-0 half-time lead before a John Evans double completed the rout.

For Welsh, it was a rare moment of glory in what would be an otherwise forgettable tenure as manager.

Left to right: *Billy Liddell, Jimmy Payne, Geoff Twentyman, Eric Anderson, Alex South, Ronnie Moran, Alan Arnell, Roy Saunders, Tom McNulty, John Evans, Brian Jackson, Alan A'Court, Ray Lambert, Doug Rudham, Phil Taylor.*

69. LIDDELLPOOL

LIVERBIRD UPON OUR CHEST

Elland Road, Leeds, Saturday 19 November 1955... a milestone occasion in Liverpool history that passed by almost unnoticed.

Recently-appointed captain Billy Liddell, ball in hand, leads the team out alongside the club's young mascot. Behind him, Roy Saunders and Doug Rudham follow on as the rest of the players prepare to make their way out of the tunnel.

Among them is debutant John Price, a Welsh full-back set to make his one and only first-team appearance.

Of greater significance is what you see on Liddell's shirt. For the first-time ever, the famous red jersey has a Liverbird displayed on the chest.

Previously, a crest had only appeared on the away shirt, and although this reincarnation of the club's iconic symbol arrived without warning, it was to become a permanent feature.

Encased in a white oval patch, with a red ring around it and the initials L.F.C. underneath, it would adorn the home shirt in this guise for the next 13 years.

As for the actual match, Don Welsh's side travelled to Yorkshire seeking their first away win of the season and they made a promising start. Liddell opened the scoring from the penalty spot before Alan Arnell doubled the advantage inside 17 minutes.

Unfortunately, when Leeds mounted a comeback Liverpool capitulated and the hosts eventually overturned the deficit to run out 4-2 winners.

It had been an inauspicious start for the new badge but the Liverbird had well and truly landed.

'GIVE IT TO BILLY'

Liverpool's 'Flying Scotsman' hurtles down the wing at Craven Cottage as George Kay's red machine powers towards another win during an unbeaten start to the 1949/50 campaign.

In what was the first-ever league meeting between Liverpool and Fulham, it was man-of-the-match Billy Liddell who proved the difference between the two sides on this day.

He scored the only goal of the game in the 15th minute – the fifth of 19 he would register that season – and the match report in that evening's *Football Echo* was not wrong when describing him as the 'greatest winger in the game today'.

Although Fulham piled on the pressure after falling behind, a stern defensive display by the Reds kept them at bay and if anyone was going to score a second, Liddell was the most likely source.

The moment captured here shows Liverpool's number 11 in full flow as he prepares to whip in a cross for Albert Stubbins; a combination of pace and power taking him beyond the reach of full-back Harry Freeman, who is left trailing in his wake and chasing shadows.

On this occasion, Liddell's magic was to no avail and the home crowd breathed a sigh of relief.

Yet for the supporters who packed onto the terracing that ran along the side of the pitch and those who risked possible injury by perching themselves perilously on top of the advertising hoardings that backed onto the River Thames, to see such artistry close up would have been worth the admission fee alone.

And it's for this reason that 'Give it to Billy' was a familiar and popular shout whenever and wherever Liverpool played back then.

Billy Liddell collected many mementos during the course of his lengthy and illustrious career but one of the more unusual items is this suitcase he received during the club's visit to Canada in 1948.

It was given to him after Liverpool's match with Ulster United at the Maple Leaf Stadium in Toronto on 15 June.

Liddell was no stranger to the city, having played there during the war as a guest for the Toronto Scottish club, and it's their president Jimmy Peden who makes the presentation.

Ray Lambert, Phil Taylor, Jim Harley and George Kay are among those looking on at a scene that wouldn't be out of place in a gangster movie.

Despite earlier scoring in a 5-1 win, Liddell thankfully didn't end up sleeping with the fishes, which is just as well because he was one of the greatest players in Liverpool history.

A league champion and cup finalist in 1947 and 1950 respectively, he later became such an influential figure at the club that the team were commonly referred to as 'Liddellpool'.

A Scotland international, he was also one of only two players to twice represent Great Britain and his fame spread far and wide. In the early 1950s he was even the target of an audacious transfer bid from a team in Colombia.

Unwaveringly loyal to the Liverpool cause, Liddell remained a one-club man and his 537 first-team appearances set a new record at the time.

As for the suitcase, it was brought home from the tour and is now stored safely in the club archives.

HEAD BOY

With Billy Liddell in the team there was always hope, yet there were also times when even the undisputed idol of all Liverpudlians in the 1950s was unable to rescue the Reds.

Even though this picture suggests Liddell could seemingly leap higher than the Main Stand, this was one of those occasions.

It's mid-January 1953 and the club's fortunes are on a worrying downward spiral. A run of 10 games without a win had sent them plummeting down the table, while a humiliating FA Cup exit at the hands of Gateshead set the alarms bells ringing even louder.

The visit to Anfield of Manchester City, the team rooted firmly to the bottom of the league and yet to win away from home, was expected to offer some much-needed respite.

Sammy Smyth, a £12,000 signing from Stoke on New Year's Eve, made his home debut but it was 'King Billy' who Kopites continued to pin their hopes of salvation on.

A wizard of the wing with thunder in his boots, Liddell, as he shows here, also possessed awesome aerial strength, which for someone who reportedly wore a size 19-inch collared shirt should perhaps come as no surprise.

The City defence are helpless to prevent the Reds' number eleven getting his head on the end of this Laurie Hughes cross but his effort unfortunately goes wide of the goal.

In what was a scrappy game, the destiny of the points was decided by a disputed Johnny Hart goal for the visitors, midway through the second half. It was a result that left Liverpool in 15th place, just five above City. Come the end of the season, relegation was only avoided with a win on the final day. It was just a pre-cursor to the increasingly inevitable.

LIVERPOOL
FOOTBALL CLUB

BRINGING HISTORY TO LIFE

***GEORGE CHILVERS** explains how his obsession with colourising pictures began – and the steps he takes to show us all what fans of the past saw*

WHERE IT BEGAN...

It's 1961, in a typical Liverpool semi-detached, and a 10-year-old football fanatic is lying on his bedroom floor leafing through his treasured football annuals.

He analyses each black and white image with an almost obsessive fervour and consults his favourite Christmas present *Letts Association Football Diary,* which lists every league club and the colours they wear. He knows them all by heart, but he checks again to make sure.

He knows the colours that are worn in the photo, but something is still missing to bring the picture to life clearly in his mind, so he reaches for his coloured pencils and starts to colour in the picture, quite roughly, but enough to get the idea.

It was that simple. That 10-year-old was me and this is how I started.

Of course, I grew up, got a job, had a family, bought a house, and all those things limited the time available to me. Not that I would swap them. But that desire to know never went away.

***Here we go!:** Liverpool-supporting ladies on their way to Wembley for the 1950 FA Cup final.*

Then much later another interest arose. Home computing became a reality, and Spectrums and Amigas led on to PCs.

The icing was added to the cake when I acquired a copy of Photoshop. Pictures could be manipulated and enhanced. But best of all, I learned how to add colour to black and white images. I remember clearly one of the first images I ever added colour to was a World War I soldier, a vaguely distant cousin who died sadly just three months before the Armistice, aged only 20. I added colour – basically a flesh tone for the face, brown hair, khaki uniform, brass buttons. It

'ONE OF THE FIRST IMAGES I ADDED COLOUR TO WAS A WORLD WAR I SOLDIER. IT WAS VERY SIMPLE COMPARED TO WHAT YOU WILL SEE IN THIS BOOK. BUT HE SPRANG TO LIFE AND I WAS HOOKED'

was very simple compared to what you will see here in this book. But he sprang to life, and I was hooked.

While I was still working, time remained precious, but retirement in 2011 freed me up, late in life, to really go for it. I could improve techniques, learn the subtleties of blending, manage saturations and opacities, and at the end of the day I just produced colourised images – just as I had 60 years ago on my bedroom floor.

WHAT IT INVOLVES...

For those of a certain age, you might remember the treat of having a box of Quality Street and holding up the coloured cellophane wrappers in

Up for the challenge: *Bob Paisley and Bill Jones in the thick of the action away to Huddersfield Town in November 1950.*

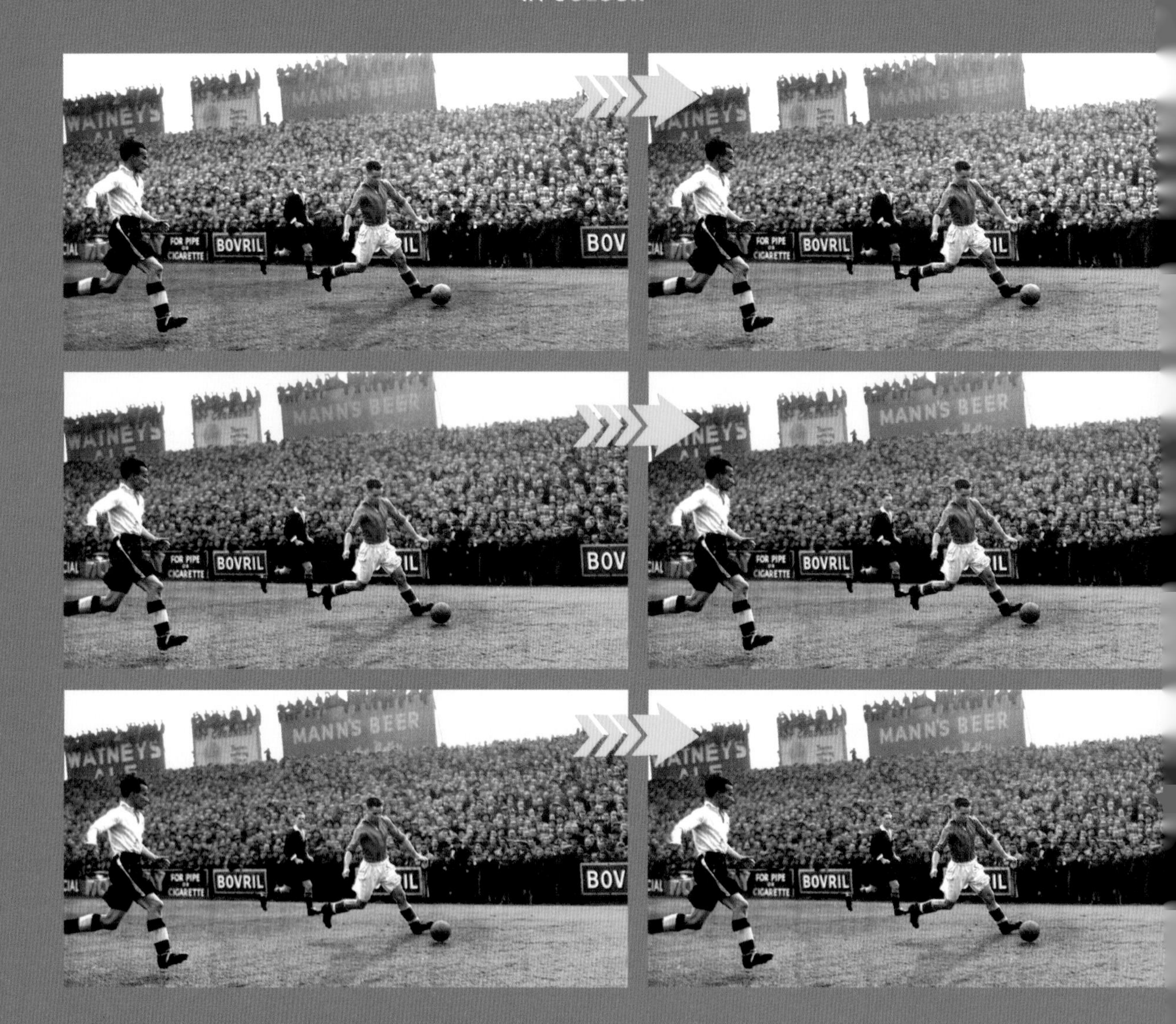

front of the black and white TV to 'make a colour TV'.

Green cellophane was great for looking at football. The pitch glowed bright green, but of course the players' faces looked like the Incredible Hulk. Or red wrappers gave a healthy glow to players' faces, but the game was played on a field of blood.

Essentially, when I colourise, I am placing a digital piece of cellophane over the picture. I tint it rather than paint over it. It's an adjustment of the hue of those areas with

'I CAREFULLY SELECT AREAS. SLOWLY, LAYER AFTER LAYER OF DIFFERENT COLOURS BUILD UP UNTIL WE HAVE THE WHOLE IMAGE IN COLOUR'

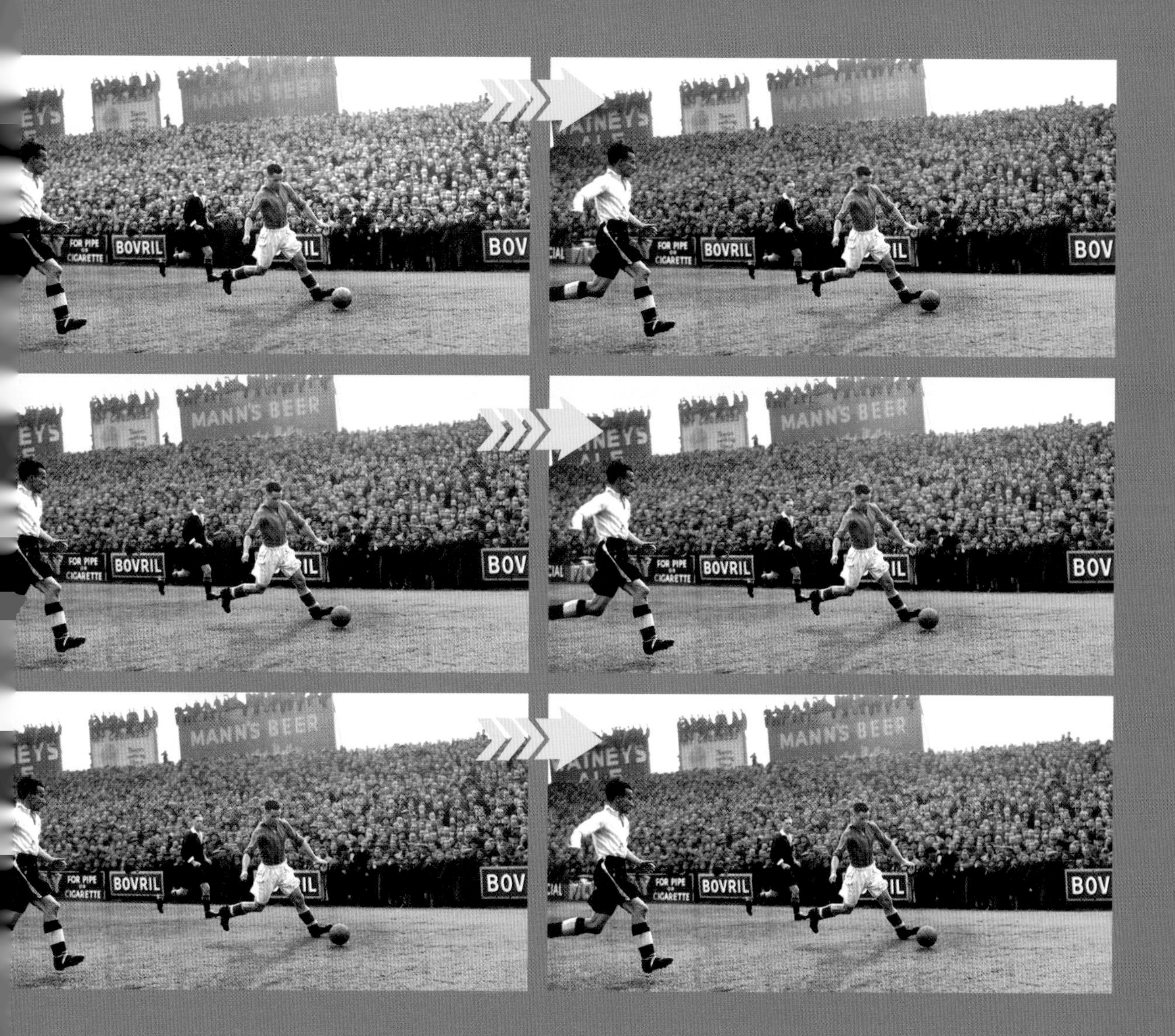

the picture still shining through, rather than a thick opaque layer of paint.

It's a simplistic explanation that is rather like saying Rembrandt put paint on a brush and slapped it on a canvas. I'm not comparing my work with Rembrandt's, of course, but knowing the simple mechanical process is one thing. Putting it together and blending it is something different. AI colourising programmes can do the basic mechanics. They do, however, completely miss the detail. And they are terrible with football pictures.

I carefully select areas. I select the grass areas and tint them green, I select Liverpool shirts and tint them red (if it's the home shirt of course), I select skin areas and tint them a flesh colour. Slowly, layer after layer of different colours build up until we have the whole image in colour.

There are huge subtleties. Foregrounds are bright and sharp, backgrounds are muted. Close up crowds have a variety of faces and colours, a distant crowd has a certain familiar look.

I have learned better ways of doing things over the last 10 years and have even improved techniques while working on this project. You're never too old to learn.

People ask how long it takes, and my standard response includes the words 'piece of string'. A very basic portrait can take just a couple of hours. Bigger and more complex pictures take much longer, spread over days, and in some cases weeks. I usually have a few pictures on the go at once to allay tedium or RSI injury.

I am my own biggest critic, and one of the most difficult things is to decide a picture is 'finished'. For this project I have had to do that. Mark Platt's feedback has been invaluable in this. Somehow, we have got to over 130 finished pictures.

'I AM MY OWN BIGGEST CRITIC, AND ONE OF THE MOST DIFFICULT THINGS IS TO DECIDE A PICTURE IS 'FINISHED"

The other regular question is: how do you know what colours to use?

Obviously skies are blue and grass is green. But depending on when in the year the picture is taken, what the weather was like, whether it was muddy or rainy, or whether the picture is in daylight or floodlit, the tones alter.

There are great websites around that can confirm shirt colours, and newspaper articles can help, and sometimes provide surprises (the 1950

Pre-match formalities: *Billy Liddell lines up alongside the Osasuna captain and match officials during the club's post-season tour to Spain in May 1958.*

Cold calling: *Skipper Ron Yeats shakes hands with his opposite number in Reykjavik ahead of Liverpool's first-ever game in European competition.*

FA Cup final socks are a good example of this).

Crowd scenes, or players in ordinary suits provide their own challenges. Obviously, I can't say definitely that a particular suit is brown or black, but I can give a good, best guess. I shamelessly use the research done by the producers of *Peaky Blinders* or *Downton Abbey* to see what colours were en vogue at a particular time.

I even try to hunt out adverts to get them right, and Mark and I have had great discussions about seat colours and paintwork around the stadium.

I hope you enjoy these pictures, seeing as near as we can what the photographer saw at the time. The colour brings out personalities, and gives character, not just to the players, but to the crowds. And, quite possibly, one person in that crowd could be your great-grandad!

I hope I have done justice to their memory.

ENGLAND'S

ROAD TO RECOVERY...1956-59

70. A SCOUSER IN OUR TEAM

A local lad from the Scotland Road area, Jimmy Melia emerged from the youth ranks in the mid-1950s to become a leading light in the club's obsessive quest for a top-flight return.

An intelligent and productive inside-forward, Melia's name was well-known in local football circles way before he made his bow in Liverpool's senior side.

As a schoolboy, he captained the city team, represented his country and had long been touted for a career in the professional game.

He joined Liverpool as an amateur in 1953, turned professional the following year and within another 12 months was running out in front of the Kop as a first-team player.

Brimming with natural talent and displaying the confidence to complement it, even as an 18-year-old Melia seemed destined to make the grade.

His debut came at home to Nottingham Forest in December 1955, and it could hardly have gone any better. He set up one goal, scored another and was unanimously hailed as man-of-the-match.

After completing his national service, Melia fully established himself as a regular in the team and also on the scoresheet.

Although slight of frame, he packed power in his boots and top scored for the club with 21 goals in 1958/59.

Despite all this, the frustration of failure to win promotion meant when supporters looked for a scapegoat Melia often found himself in the firing line.

His best season in a red shirt, though, would ironically come in the season Liverpool's First Division exile finally ended.

71. ROAD RUNNERS

New manager Phil Taylor, partly hidden on the far left, watches on in the Anfield car park in 1956 as the Liverpool squad embark on a pre-season road run.

Former captain and coach Taylor had been promoted to the top job in the wake of Don Welsh's sacking at the end of the previous campaign.

With the terraced houses of Lake Street behind them, new signing Tommy Younger leads from the front alongside club captain Billy Liddell, while other players of note are future backroom stalwarts Ronnie Moran and Geoff Twentyman.

Also pictured are three young players who would go on to enjoy fairly successful careers as First Division managers away from Anfield in the 1980s, Jimmy Melia, Bobby Campbell and Keith Burkinshaw, plus a teenage Johnny Morrissey,

who would later find fame at Everton after a controversial move across Stanley Park in 1962.

The destination for this run was the club's training ground but, on the pitch, it was to be an all too familiar story for the Reds, a case of 'if only'.

After a poor start, which saw them collect just 11 points from their opening 12 games and left them languishing in 14th place, Taylor's team recovered well enough and eventually fought their way into the race for promotion.

Unfortunately, come the final reckoning they were left to rue those earlier poor results as they agonisingly missed out on a place in the top two by a solitary point.

It was the closest they would come to regaining their top-flight status during Taylor's four years as boss.

72. THIS IS MELWOOD

Out in the leafy suburb of West Derby during the summer of 1956, preparations for the new season are well underway at the club's Melwood training ground.

Situated just four miles from the hustle and bustle of Anfield, this seemingly tranquil setting was originally the home of playing fields that belonged to St Francis Xavier College.

The site had been acquired by the club six years earlier and its name derived from the surnames of the two schoolmasters who orchestrated the sale, Fathers Melling and Woodlock.

Although not yet fully developed – the old cricket pavilions can still be seen in the background – it was to prove a visionary move.

Melwood became the place where the long hours of hard work were put in on a daily basis during the week; a refuge from prying eyes where training methods and tactical ideas could blossom.

In his new role on the coaching staff, Bob Paisley can be seen taking charge of such a session, with skipper Billy Liddell leading the way in this heading drill.

Waiting their turn, from left to right, are half-back and future chief scout Geoff Twentyman, striker John Evans – one of only a handful of players to score five goals in a game for Liverpool – goalkeeper Tommy Younger, a Scotland international recently signed from Hibernian, and vice-captain Laurie Hughes.

While the coming season would be Evans' last at the club, Liddell, Twentyman, Younger and Hughes would be key players in the team in the coming years.

LFC

73. LIVERPOOL V LIVERPOOL

The one fixture Liverpool could never lose...it's the 'Reds' versus the 'Whites' in the annual public trial match at Anfield in August 1956.

Viewed back then as the traditional curtain-raiser to the new season, this was the final dress rehearsal before the following week's big kick-off.

It was an opportunity for any last-minute plans to be fine-tuned and for players to convince the selection committee that they were deserving of a place in the first eleven.

For supporters, it was a chance to gauge the team's prospects for the coming months and catch a first glimpse of any new signings.

On this occasion, Tommy Younger was the only notable new face, while fellow goalkeeper Doug Rudham was one of the players out to impress.

Rudham held the unwanted distinction of being the keeper that conceded nine goals in the club's all-time heaviest defeat and had dropped down the pecking order following Younger's arrival.

Within seconds of the first whistle, the South African stopper can be seen diving bravely at the feet of Billy Liddell, while the promising Dick White, recruited from Scunthorpe the previous year, looks on.

As expected, it was the Reds who ran out winners. Liddell was among the scorers, grabbing a hat-trick in a 6-1 victory.

While Liddell went on to play in all but one game in 1956/57, Rudham and White had to make do with just two and five first-team appearances respectively.

White's time would come though, and he'd eventually become Liverpool captain. Rudham remained at the club for a further four years.

74. CAMPBELL CROCKED

Defender Don Campbell puts his body on the line in an attempt to make a last-ditch challenge away at Stoke City in January 1957.

A lesser-known figure in the club's history, Campbell unfortunately suffered an injury in the incident, and it was to ultimately affect the outcome of this Second Division fixture.

An England youth international from Bootle, he initially joined the Reds in 1950 and made his debut in the 1953/54 season.

His appearance here at the Victoria Ground, however, was his first in the senior side for almost two years, recalled as a replacement for the injured Geoff Twentyman.

With both teams in the hunt for promotion, the game was of vital importance, and it drew a crowd of 31,144, a figure that included a fair number of Liverpool fans.

In what was a lively encounter, Campbell had his work cut out and not even a combination of him and Ronnie Moran could stop winger Neville Coleman from playing a dangerous ball across the goalmouth.

Fortunately, it didn't lead to a goal, but Campbell needed treatment on his thigh. The injury restricted his mobility, so he was later moved to outside-right and then centre-forward, leaving the team disjointed.

The destiny of the points was eventually decided in the 77th minute by a headed goal from home striker Harry Oscroft. The result left Liverpool in fifth place, while Stoke moved up into second, although neither side would eventually be promoted.

Campbell went on to make a further 33 appearances in the first team before he was transferred to Crewe Alexandra in July 1958.

75. THAT OLD CUP MAGIC

A picture that encapsulates how much the FA Cup meant. It's 8 January 1958 and the final whistle has just blown on Liverpool's third round replay away to Southend United.

Supporters spill onto the pitch in celebration following a five-goal thriller at Roots Hall and it's the travelling Liverpudlians who are smiling.

After a 1-1 draw at Anfield four days earlier, the teams met again on a Wednesday afternoon and the odds of an upset were high. Liverpool had history with their Third Division opponents, having been shocked by them at the same stage of the competition just the season before.

On home soil, Southend were confident of a repeat performance, but the visitors couldn't have made a better start, with full-back John Molyneux netting his first goal for the club in the opening minute.

Later in the half, Molyneux unfortunately scored at the opposite end to cancel out his earlier effort and then, on the stroke of the interval, the home side took the lead.

With 11 minutes remaining the score was still the same and Liverpool were facing the prospect of another FA Cup humiliation. Then came the real drama and in the space of three frantic minutes the tie was turned on its head.

Dick White began the revival when heading in the equaliser before Tony Rowley finished off a fine move to hammer home what proved to be the winner.

As Billy Liddell is mobbed on his way to the tunnel, the joy on the faces of these Liverpool fans, the majority of whom are grown men, is plain to see. The FA Cup really was the greatest knockout competition in the world back then.

MARTINI

76. FROZEN IN TIME

Dick White and Geoff Twentyman lurk in the background as Ronnie Moran attempts to cut out the threat of an opposition attack. Don't be fooled by the colours, this is Liverpool playing at home in a 1958 FA Cup tie.

Northampton Town of the Third Division South are the visitors to a snow-covered Anfield and a place in the fifth round is the prize at stake.

Whenever a colour clash occurred in the competition during this era it was not unknown for both teams to wear their change strips.

Having worn blue when defeating Arsenal in the previous round, Northampton were hoping it would be a lucky omen against a Liverpool side that sat third in Division Two.

Interest in the tie was huge and for what was the first-ever meeting between the two clubs, 56,939 braved the cold, including 8,000 travelling supporters.

With the pitch having only been passed as playable two hours prior to kick-off, a layer of melting ice was still visible when the game got underway, and the tricky conditions are clear to see as Moran attempts to close down Northampton's Jack English.

It all combined to increase the risk of a cup upset and until near the end it was a close affair. All-square at half-time, Barry Hawkings levelled for the spirited visitors after Billy Liddell opened the scoring, and it wasn't until the 79th minute that Liverpool regained the lead.

It came via an own goal from Ben Collins and minutes later Louis Bimpson put the outcome beyond doubt. Scunthorpe were beaten in the next round but Liverpool's cup hopes were ended at Blackburn in the quarter-final.

77. WORCESTER SORES

Dick White holds his head in his hands, while John Molyneux and Tommy Younger begin their inquest into how an early goal has been conceded during an infamous FA Cup tie at Worcester City in 1959.

Only nine minutes had elapsed at St George's Lane and Liverpool were already teetering on the brink of what would be the lowest point in their on-field history.

Southern League Worcester had never before reached the third round of the competition and while the Reds' FA Cup pedigree was hardly one to shout about, Phil Taylor's Second Division side were big favourites.

The game, postponed the previous weekend due to a frozen pitch, was scheduled for a Thursday afternoon, but in front of a record home crowd of 15,000, conditions were still far from ideal.

On a notoriously sloping pitch that was devoid of grass, Worcester took the lead through Tommy Skuse following a defensive mix-up between Molyneux and Younger.

Rocked by the incident, Liverpool failed to recover and became more desperate as the clock ticked towards full-time. Ten minutes from the end another mistake compounded the misery when White mis-directed an intended clearance over the head of Younger and into his own net.

A late Geoff Twentyman penalty was scant consolation. The damage had been done and this was undoubtedly the most humiliating cup exit Liverpool had ever suffered.

On the plus side, if there could be one, it was to prove the catalyst for change at a club that had been stagnating for too long.

5
2

78. TOP-NOTCH A'COURT

Alan A'Court nets from an acute angle at Swansea in the opening minute of Liverpool's final game of the 1958/59 season.

But the grey skies and wide open spaces on the Vetch Field terraces paint a scene as bleak as the Reds' campaign had been.

Another near miss in the race for promotion had been confirmed weeks before this concluding fixture and was the cause of yet more exasperation among the club's long-suffering followers.

Earlier in the week Liverpool played their final home game of the season in front of just over 11,000, the then lowest post-war Anfield attendance.

The club's plight was becoming more worrying, and it seems remarkable that they were still able to hold on to quality players such as A'Court.

A speedy left-winger whose talents would have graced any of the great Liverpool teams, Rainhill-born A'Court was another homegrown star who displayed tremendous loyalty to the Anfield cause during this most barren of spells.

His outstanding form saw international recognition deservedly come his way and, despite plying his trade in Division Two, he represented England at the 1958 World Cup.

Several top-flight clubs declared an interest in him but A'Court was never tempted. This devotion to his boyhood club would eventually be rewarded, but not until late in his career.

As for the stunning goal he scored here, it was one of 63 he registered for the Reds. Although it deserved to win the game, on this occasion it didn't, and Liverpool had to settle for a 3-3 draw.

BIRTH OF THE BOOTROOM

Club captain Johnny Wheeler extends a welcoming handshake to new first-team coach Reuben Bennett upon his arrival at Anfield in November 1958.

Manager Phil Taylor, Billy Liddell, Jimmy Harrower and Laurie Hughes also turn out to greet the man brought in to help revolutionise the team's training regime.

Born in Aberdeen and a former goalkeeper with Hull City, Queen of the South and Dundee, Bennett's reputation as a coach had been cultivated during spells at Dundee, again, Motherwell and Third Lanark, plus a spell as manager of Ayr United.

When a coaching vacancy arose at Anfield, chairman TV Williams head-hunted Bennett and his capture was viewed as a major coup.

A tough, craggy Scot, he had been a physical training instructor in the army and was renowned for being a fitness fanatic.

Once the formalities of his appointment were out of the way he immediately got down to business and was soon working the players vigorously at Melwood.

The results may not have been evident straight away but over time Liverpool would reap the rewards of the decision to recruit the hugely popular Bennett.

Crucially, he gelled with the existing backroom team and those who would soon join. Together, they helped build one of the most revered dynasties in football and Reuben Bennett would remain a vital part of that for the next three decades.

80. SMOKIN' JOE

A 36-year-old Joe Fagan reports to Anfield in July 1958 ready for the first day of work in his new job.

The Liverpool-born former Manchester City defender had been recruited from Rochdale as the club's new assistant trainer.

He'd been brought in to succeed the departing Dickie Dorsett and the appointment, when officially announced two months earlier, was a low-key affair.

Unassuming, down-to-earth, and never one to court publicity, it's exactly how Fagan would have wanted it.

With the new role at Liverpool came a new house, a neat and tidy semi-detached in nearby Lynholme Road, meaning he didn't have far to walk for work.

In addition to his previous position as Harry Catterick's assistant at Rochdale, he had also enjoyed a successful spell as player-manager of Nelson.

Among his many duties at Anfield, Fagan was entrusted with nurturing the club's young talent and was responsible for running the reserve team.

Nicknamed 'Smokin' Joe' due to his fondness for the odd cigarette, Fagan also had an integral part to play in the creation of Anfield's now legendary Bootroom – a place his name would become synonymous with over the coming years.

81. THE MESSIAH

The would-be Anfield messiah surveys his new kingdom as he maps out his grand plans for the club's future.

From the steep concrete steps at the back of the Spion Kop, Bill Shankly looks out onto Walton Breck Road and towards the Albert pub, across the rooftops of the cramped terrace streets and off into the distance.

He felt instantly at home; this was his type of place. Those that lived here were his type of people and he had only one thing on his mind: to make them happy.

The former Carlisle, Grimsby, Workington and Huddersfield boss had been announced as Liverpool's fourth post-war manager on 1 December 1959 and officially assumed control a fortnight later.

Shankly breezed into Anfield like a breath of fresh air and a local journalist was suitably impressed enough to write: "The new manager's confidence and firm resolve are infectious. Nobody can be in his company for more than a few minutes and not realise that here is a driving force who will not spare himself pains to get the job he has in view."

He was taking charge of a club that had been lying dormant in Division Two for far too long. His brief was simple: to return Liverpool to the promised land of the top-flight.

His ambitions stretched much further than that though. He wanted to build a team so good that it would be capable of 'conquering the bloody world'.

There can be no denying that the task he faced was a massive one but by drawing on the passion of the crowd he was well aware of the untapped potential within the club. What he had to do first, was provide them with a team to be proud of.

82. SHANKLY'S PRIDE

This is the first known photograph to feature Bill Shankly with his Liverpool team.

It was published in the *Echo* on the morning of the club's FA Cup third round tie at home to Leyton Orient in January 1960.

Three weeks earlier Shankly's first game in charge had resulted in a 4-0 Anfield defeat against Cardiff, while a 3-0 loss at Charlton then followed.

Fortunes did slowly begin to improve and two Roger Hunt goals, scored in the first and last minutes, were enough to secure a 2-1 victory over Orient.

Liverpool's cup run went no further than the next round though and they again missed out on promotion, this time finishing eight points off the top two.

Shankly knew he had the foundations of a decent team but the squad he inherited was in desperate need of an overhaul.

Within weeks of his arrival, he had drawn up a list of 24 names that he deemed surplus to requirements. A year later they were all gone, and it didn't stop there.

While some of the players pictured would have a key role to play in the early stages of the Reds revival, by the time Shankly led the club to a first-ever FA Cup triumph in 1965, the squad had undergone such a massive transformation that only two of the 14 remained.

***Back row (left to right):** Roger Hunt, Fred Morris, John Molyneux, Dick White, Bert Slater, Johnny Wheeler, Geoff Twentyman, Tommy Leishman, Jimmy Harrower.*
***Front row:** Alan A'Court, Bobby Campbell, Dave Hickson, Ronnie Moran (captain), Bill Shankly, Jimmy Melia.*

83. THREE WISE MEN

A meeting of three great footballing minds. Bill Shankly, Bob Paisley and Joe Fagan; modest men with knowledge in abundance, talking tactics and pulling together for the Liverpool cause.

Of all the decisions Shankly made when he took charge at Anfield, arguably his most important was to retain the existing backroom team, of which Paisley and Fagan were key figures.

Each of the esteemed trio came from similar working-class backgrounds and had played professionally at the highest level.

Collectively, they shared the same beliefs on how the game should be played. Their philosophy was one borne out of simplicity; find the nearest red shirt, pass and move. It was a trait that would define the team's style of play for years to come.

Known as the 'Liverpool Way', it was cultivated at Melwood, where revolutionary games of one and two-touch five-a-sides replaced the monotony of energy-sapping road runs.

They are pictured here in Weybridge, near London, during a training session the day before the 1965 FA Cup final.

What words of wisdom were being spoken we'll never know but to eavesdrop on this conversation would be akin to unlocking the long lost secrets of the Bootroom.

Shankly, Paisley and Fagan, with the help of others, were instrumental in shaping the entire ethos of the club and laying down the blueprints for future success.

That the career paths of all three men crossed in the same place at the same time was, for Liverpool Football Club, the ultimate blessing.

THE GLORY DAYS RETURN...1961-69

84. READY STEADY GO!

The Reds' revival is under starter's orders and Bill Shankly is working the players hard at Melwood.

In what was the new manager's first full season in charge, Dick White is now captain. There's also a fresh face in the pack and he would have been one of the favourites to win this race.

Kevin Lewis (second from the left) had been signed from Sheffield United for what was then a joint club record fee of £13,000.

He was to enjoy a great first season in a red shirt and got off to a flying start by scoring twice on his debut in an opening-day 2-0 home win over Leeds United.

A fast and tricky winger who could also operate as an inside-forward, Lewis went on to finish as the club's top scorer.

Yet despite his 22 goals, promotion once again evaded Liverpool's clutches in 1960/61.

Another third-place finish, the fourth in six seasons, was disappointing, but the gap had been narrowed and it was generally viewed as a season of progress.

With another new addition in Gordon Milne boosting the ranks, Shankly was slowly but surely building a team capable of bridging that gap and winning the next big race – the one for promotion.

Left to right: *Dick White, Kevin Lewis, Roger Hunt, Jimmy Melia, Alan A'Court, Bill Shankly.*

85. THE COLOSSUS

There was only ever going to be one winner in this aerial battle at Boundary Park in January 1962.

He may have just been six months into his Liverpool career, but in size and stature, the Reds' number five, Ron Yeats, was already a footballing giant.

"Six foot four and strong as an ox," according to the man who signed him. On unveiling Yeats to the press, Bill Shankly described him as a 'colossus' and invited journalist to walk around him.

Along with the signing of fellow Scot, Ian St John, former slaughterman Yeats – an £18,000 capture from Dundee United – helped complete the jigsaw as Liverpool, at long last, made a concerted effort to escape the Second Division wilderness in 1961/62.

Left to right (Liverpool players only): *Gerry Byrne, Tommy Leishman, Roger Hunt, Gordon Milne, Ron Yeats, Bert Slater, Dick White, Ian Callaghan.*

The game featured here, though, offered a welcome break from the intense scrutiny of the promotion chase.

This was the fourth round of the FA Cup away to lower league Oldham; the type of banana skin Liverpool had too often slipped on in the past.

But with Yeats at his imposing and commanding best, and St John scoring twice, the Division Two leaders came through unscathed.

When tickets for the game had been put on sale at Oldham a week before, hundreds of Liverpool fans were among those who started queuing at 4am in the morning and travelling Liverpudlians eventually made up almost half of the 42,000 crowd.

The FA Cup was still of massive interest but achieving a top two finish in the league was, this season, the number one priority.

Left to right: *Tommy Leishman, Gerry Byrne (partly hidden), Alan A'Court, Ronnie Moran, Gordon Milne, Jimmy Melia.*

86. DIAMONDS IN THE MUD

Not even grey skies and incessant rain could dampen the mood of euphoria at Anfield on the day Liverpudlians celebrated confirmation of the club's long-awaited top-flight return.

When the final whistle sounded on a 2-0 home victory over Southampton in April 1962, it was the moment everyone had been waiting for since relegation eight years before.

On a quagmire of a pitch, two first-half goals from Kevin Lewis, only playing because Ian St John was serving a suspension, secured the necessary points required to end any doubt. Not that there was much.

Liverpool had led the table from the outset. Inspired by the summer arrivals of St John, for a club record £37,500, and the talismanic man mountain of a skipper 'Rowdy' Yeats, the season had been a procession from start to finish.

Such was the lead they held over their rivals, promotion, and the title, had long since been considered a formality. Both were cut and dried with five games to spare.

As the victorious team left the field, opposition players and match officials stopped to applaud them, while a jubilant crowd braved the mud to invade the pitch and refused to go home until the players came back out for a final curtain call. When they did, Yeats and St John ended up getting thrown into the Kop to join the celebrations.

It had been an Easter Saturday to remember and Liverpudlians were able to hold their heads high once again.

87. UP THE REDS

The Liverpool team celebrate in the Anfield dressing room with the club's first major piece of silverware in 15 years.

Promotion was what mattered most in 1961/62 but the Second Division Championship trophy is the icing on the cake of a triumphant season.

The presentation came after the final home game against Charlton on 30 April, but until the dying moments the champagne was in danger of going flat.

With 89 minutes on the clock the Reds trailed 1-0 and it needed one of the most dramatic rescue-acts ever witnessed at Anfield to maintain the party atmosphere.

It began with a Roger Hunt equaliser, crashed in off the underside of the bar, and was quickly followed by a well-placed strike from Alan A'Court that sparked scenes of pandemonium among the crowd.

It had been a classic smash-and-grab job, and no-one could begrudge the champions this final moment of glory.

Supporters once again poured onto the pitch in celebration and the players retreated to the directors' box where they received the trophy before the party continued down below.

It had been a campaign in which the Reds remained unbeaten at home and one that saw Hunt set a new club record for most goals scored in a season (41).

After eight long years it was finally time to say 'good riddance' to the Second Division. Phase one of Bill Shankly's masterplan was complete and an exciting new era lay ahead for the club.

Back row (left to right): *Bob Paisley (trainer), Gordon Milne, Jim Furnell, Tommy Leishman, Roger Hunt, Ian St John, Ian Callaghan.*
Front row: *Gerry Byrne, Alan A'Court, Ron Yeats, Thomas Valentine Williams (chairman), Mr Joe Richards (Football League president), Bill Shankly (manager), Jimmy Melia.*

88. MERSEY PRIDE

Kevin Lewis can't contain his delight. It's the last minute of the first Merseyside league derby in twelve seasons and Roger Hunt has just rescued a point for Liverpool.

After their eight-year exile this is the Reds back in the big time and games don't come any bigger. It's the one that supporters looked for first when the fixture list was published. 73,000 supporters packed into Goodison Park with high expectations, and they were rewarded with a spectacle befitting this most eagerly-awaited occasion in September 1962.

Lewis, a man for the big occasion yet again, had earlier cancelled out a Roy Vernon penalty that opened the scoring but after ex-Red Johnny Morrissey restored Everton's

advantage, it looked as though derby bragging rights would be going to the Blues.

Then, with just sixty seconds left on the referee's watch, Alan A'Court centred. Lewis nodded the ball down and Hunt swept it home from six yards out to equalise.

As the Everton players look at each other in despair, Lewis and Hunt celebrate against the backdrop of Goodison's old Main Stand.

It was a sensational end to a thrilling game, with four goals shared, but Liverpool the happier of the two teams.

Although the Toffees went on to claim the title that season, there was a new team in town, and this was a marker in the sand for what was to come.

89. RONNIE ON THE SPOT

A glowing Anfield erupts as Reds number three, Ronnie Moran, arms raised skywards, turns to receive the acclaim of his team-mates after converting one of the most celebrated penalties ever scored at the Kop end.

It's February 1963 and the dying seconds of extra-time in an epic FA Cup fourth-round replay against Burnley, beaten finalists the previous year and cup favourites this time around.

But in front of a near 58,000 crowd – the fifth highest attendance in Anfield history – Moran, amid unbearable tension, has just held his nerve to knock them out.

These two evenly-matched teams had drawn 1-1 at Turf Moor in the first game and the return meeting was one of the most highly anticipated cup-ties in years.

After 120 minutes under the Anfield floodlights it was 1-1 again, Ian St John, on the stroke of half-time cancelling out an earlier goal from Alex Elder.

With time almost up, there was a mix-up in the Burnley defence, St John attempted to take advantage but was dragged to the floor by 'keeper Adam Blacklaw. There was no doubting the award of a penalty.

Moran stepped back, took just a short run-up and blasted the ball as hard as he could. Blacklaw was helpless to stop it. The net bulged, the Kop exploded, and the following night's *Liverpool Echo* described it as, 'The greatest finish to any match ever played at Anfield'.

90. THE CUP DRAW

It's all ears to the wireless as Liverpool are about to discover the identity of their next opponents in the 1963 FA Cup.

Having followed up the dramatic victory over Burnley with victories over Arsenal and West Ham United, the Reds were now in the midst of their best run in the competition since last reaching the final in 1950. FA Cup fever was once again taking a firm grip of the club.

Bill Shankly, Bob Paisley and Reuben Bennett are joined by assistant club secretary Bill Barlow as they await news of the semi-final draw that is being made at the Football Association's Lancaster Gate headquarters.

It's lunchtime, training has stopped and so too has everything else. In factories, offices, homes and schools across the city it's a similar story.

The rustling of the famous velvet bag that contains the numbered balls is the first sound that can be heard over the airwaves, and it adds to the mounting tension.

Alongside Liverpool in the draw are Leicester City, Manchester United, and Southampton or Nottingham Forest, who had not yet resolved their quarter-final tie.

Shankly and his players wouldn't have said it publicly but there was one team above all others that they wanted to avoid and it's the one they are paired with.

The first ball out of the bag was the one representing Liverpool, followed by the team they had already lost twice against in the league that season, Leicester City; a meeting of the joint cup favourites.

Four weeks later Liverpool's worst fears became reality and a solitary Mike Stringfellow goal at Hillsborough brought their gallant cup run to a heart-breaking conclusion.

91. FAB FOUR

Ian St John, Ron Yeats, Ken Dodd and Billy Liddell – four of the most famous names the city of Liverpool has ever known.

Nowhere did the contrasting cultures of football and showbiz collide more in the mid-1960s than at Liverpool Football Club.

It was an era when local musicians took the pop charts by storm, when almost every voice on television had a Scouse accent and when Bill Shankly's Liverpool sprung into international consciousness.

No surprise then that the city was famously described at the time as 'the centre of the universe'.

But while The Beatles, Merseyside's most famous exports, declared no allegiance when it came to football, other celebrities were only too pleased to associate themselves with the Reds, among them comedian Ken Dodd.

On this photograph, taken in December 1963, Dodd links up with Liverpool stars Ian St John, Ron Yeats and the recently-retired Billy Liddell to impersonate the 'Fab Four'.

With the Kop Choir as their backing singers, who knows, they may have had a number one hit on their hands.

The cover of Sgt Pepper's Lonely Hearts Club Band by The Beatles, released in 1967, featured former Liverpool star Albert Stubbins – another example of the link between showbiz and the club

92. EE-AYE-ADDIO WE'VE WON THE CURLETT CUP

Bill Shankly and his newly-crowned champions take a bow from the front row of the directors' box while proudly showing off perhaps the most unusual and cherished trophy in the club's collection.

Liverpool had just clinched the First Division title by beating Arsenal 5-0, but with the actual league championship trophy not being on site it was time to improvise.

Fortunately, two supporters had thought similarly and during the week had got to work on a makeshift memento to commemorate the crowning moment of the Reds' glorious march to success in 1963/64.

Using an old vase of their grandmother's, brothers Terry and Teddy Curlett painted it red and white, plastered it with pictures of the team and used the top of a staircase balustrade to make the lid. They then brought it with them to Anfield on the day. And what a day it turned out to be.

With four games of the season left to play, the Reds required just a point to secure the club's sixth league title success and excitement among Liverpudlians was at fever pitch.

Amid a carnival atmosphere, the Kop choir treated BBC's *Panorama* cameras to a full repertoire of their favourite hits, from 'She Loves You' to 'When The Reds Go Marching In'.

Inspired by this pre-match revelry, Liverpool came flying out of the starting blocks. Ian St John opened the scoring after just seven minutes and Alf Arrowsmith made it 2-0 before the break. The second half was a stroll, with three further goals added courtesy of Peter Thompson (2) and Roger Hunt.

As the players embarked on their victorious lap of honour 'Ee-aye-addio we've won the league' bellowed around the ground, and even though it wasn't the real trophy that was being paraded, Anfield had never witnessed such scenes of jubilation.

The homemade cup reappeared when the club next won the title, but it then went into storage until it was donated to the club museum, where it's now on display and has been christened the 'Curlett Cup' after the brothers who created it.

Left to right: *Peter Thompson, Ian Callaghan, Alf Arrowsmith, Bill Shankly, Ron Yeats, Tommy Lawrence, Gerry Byrne, Roger Hunt.*

Back row (left to right): *Phil Chisnall, Ian St John, Tommy Smith, Ron Yeats, Bob Paisley (trainer), Chris Lawler, TV Williams (chairman), Willie Stevenson, Reuben Bennett (coach), Trevor Roberts, Tommy Lawrence, Harry Latham (director), Phil Ferns, Fred Molyneux.*
Front row: *Alan A'Court, Alf Arrowsmith, Ian Callaghan, Gerry Byrne, Ed Sullivan (TV host), Bobby Graham, Gordon Wallace, Ronnie Moran.*

93. THE BOYS FROM BEATLESVILLE

The fame of Liverpool Football Club was starting to spread far and wide by 1964, as proved by their TV appearance in May that year on the famous *Ed Sullivan Show* in New York.

Following in the footsteps of those other famous sons of the city, The Beatles, Liverpool travelled Stateside at the end of their title-winning season.

Three months earlier John, Paul, George and Ringo had performed six times on the same stage that the squad are pictured on here.

During what was the club's fourth visit to the USA, another Liverpudlian band, Gerry & The Pacemakers, the one responsible for Anfield's now famous anthem, were also due to appear on the *Ed Sullivan Show* and it was arranged for the squad to be among the guests.

Earlier in the day, Liverpool had recorded a 7-1 victory over New York Metropolitan All-Stars at Randall's Island in their second match of a 10-game tour. They then headed to Broadway to enjoy the live broadcast, not expecting that, midway through, the spotlight would fall on them.

"We are delighted tonight to have in our audience one of the great soccer teams of England, the Liverpool team that won the English league title," Sullivan told his viewers as the camera panned onto the players in the crowd. "Would you stand up gentlemen, all of you, everybody up," he added. "Come on America, let's hear it for Liverpool."

Although relatively unknown in this part of the world the team were inundated with autograph requests and invited on stage for a picture.

At the time, there was no more popular show on American television than the one hosted every Sunday evening by Ed Sullivan and an estimated 70 million viewers are believed to have tuned into this episode.

94. CHARITY BEGINS AT HOME

Two of the most iconic and successful captains of the Sixties share the spoils in the aftermath of the 1964 Charity Shield at Anfield.

Liverpool's Ron Yeats and West Ham's Bobby Moore were no strangers to lifting silverware during this era.

Between them, they skippered their respective sides, including England in the case of the latter, to no fewer than seven trophies between 1962 and 1966.

Yeats won two league titles, the Second Division championship and FA Cup. Moore claimed the FA Cup, European Cup Winners' Cup and World Cup.

It was perhaps fitting then that when league champions Liverpool and FA Cup holders West Ham United clashed in the season's annual curtain-raiser, both clubs got to hold the silverware for six months.

Ten years before the fixture was moved to Wembley, it was traditionally held on the ground of the champions, but despite home advantage on this occasion the Reds had to settle for a draw.

Twice they took the lead, first through Gordon Wallace and then Gerry Byrne, but twice they were pegged back. John Byrne and Geoff Hurst replied for the visitors.

In the days before penalty shoot-outs were even a thing, it meant both sides settled for taking turns (six months each) to display the shield in their trophy cabinet.

Although considered nothing more than a glorified friendly, there was still some prestige attached to the game and it was another honour, albeit shared, to add to the list.

More importantly, for both clubs, it was the prelude to what would be another successful season.

95. SAINT IAN'S WEMBLEY WINNER

Liverpool history is made as Ian St John's Wembley header wins the club's first-ever FA Cup in 1965.

It brought to an end 73 years of despair in a competition Liverpudlians had longed to see their team succeed in more than any other.

Many believed they would never live to experience this moment and it was a longstanding joke that if the Reds did ever win the FA Cup, the Liver Birds would fly from their perch, never to return.

Beneath the twin towers on 1 May, a tense battle ensued.

It was deep into the second period of extra-time. Billy Bremner had cancelled out Roger Hunt's opener and with the score locked at 1-1 a replay at Maine Road was looking increasingly likely.

Then Ian Callaghan floated a ball in from the right, over the head of the advancing Leeds 'keeper Gary Sprake.

St John, socks down by his ankles, and straining every sinew in his body, seized the opportunity and seemed to twist in mid-air as he leapt towards it. With a nod of the head, he directed the ball goalwards. Paul Reaney, motionless on the line, was helpless to prevent it going in and Liverpudlians, no matter where

they were in the world, simultaneously erupted with joy.

Only nine minutes remained and there were no further goals. The hoodoo that had hung heavily over the club for so long had been buried once and for all.

All that was left was to see Ron Yeats climb the famous steps and collect the coveted trophy from Queen Elizabeth II.

The sight caused an unprecedented outpouring of emotion. Grown men openly wept tears of happiness and the older generation revealed they could now die happy. No goal had, or has, ever meant that much.

POOL
LIVERPOOL

96. VICTORIOUS AND GLORIOUS

The famous Spion Kop in all its glory acclaims the soon-to-be-crowned kings of English football in 1966.

Liverpool stand on the brink of being champions for a record-equalling seventh time.

There's an unprecedented feel-good factor swirling around Anfield and this 28,000-strong swaying mass of red and white is ready to play its part.

According to Bill Shankly these Kopites were his 12th man, capable of sucking the ball into the net and roaring the team on to another victory. They would not let him down.

In what was Liverpool's last home fixture of the campaign, just one more win was required and visitors Chelsea showed their respect by forming a guard of honour for the champions-elect as the players took to the field.

Although the First Division title race of that season was always a close-run affair, there was a sense of inevitability about the eventual destination of the trophy.

Shankly boasted that his players were the fittest in the country and it certainly rang true in 1965/66. He never had a more settled side. Only 14 players were called upon, a record that went unmatched until 1981.

The names tripped off the tongue. The majority were now at the peak of their careers, and two second-half goals by Roger Hunt sealed a 2-1 win.

The scarves and flags on the Kop came out again as the now familiar scenes of celebration unfolded.

97. HEY THERE HONEY WEST

A Liverpool supporter encroaches onto the pitch to hand Everton goalkeeper Gordon West his traditional gift from the Kop during the Merseyside derby of September 1967.

Opposition 'keepers have always been warmly welcomed at Anfield but the relationship Kopites forged with West was particularly special.

Highly respected but habitually taunted in equal measure, they christened him 'Honey' West in reference to a fictional television character of the same name and would regularly hand over a personalised handbag to remind him.

The rapport was two-fold and in return, the Blues number one would give back as good as he got.

After being greeted with a mass two-finger salute and flurry of oranges on his first derby appearance in front of the Kop, West proceeded to keep a clean sheet and wasn't slow in letting the crowd know.

He would play up to the Liverpool fans each season and, in turn, Kopites continued to revel in their friendly ridiculing of him, even rewording a popular song of the time in his honour.

To the tune of 'Hey There Georgy Girl', a 1967 hit by The Seekers, West would be serenaded with lyrics that compared him with 'Georgie Best' and joked at his expense.

It was a show of gratitude laced with a cutting edge, but like with the handbag, it was just part and parcel of derby day banter from a bygone era.

ONEY
VEST
A B C D

98. 'HE MUST WISH THE GROUND WOULD OPEN UP'

The most famous own goal in Merseyside derby history. Goodison Park, 6 December 1969. A moment in time that will have forever haunted Everton's Sandy Brown.

It came in the 54th minute of a match the hosts were big favourites to win. Top of the league, unbeaten at home and the highest scorers in the division, Harry Catterick's Blues were heading towards the title and if you believed the hype, Liverpool were crossing the park only to make up the numbers.

But following a goalless first half, Emlyn Hughes broke the deadlock shortly after the restart. Then, just seven minutes later, came the goal Liverpudlians will never tire of replaying.

Peter Thompson cut in from the left wing and delivered a cross that evaded the clutches of 'keeper Gordon West.

Brown, tracking back, managed to get his head under the ball but could only direct it upwards into the top corner of an unguarded goal.

To compound his misery, it came at the Park End of the ground, in front of the vast majority of celebrating Liverpool supporters, and he cut a forlorn-looking figure as he slumped to his knees in the back of the net.

Commentating on *Match of the Day* later that night, David Coleman was typically succinct in describing the scene: "He must wish the ground would open up...poor Sandy Brown, the agony of the player in that situation."

Bobby Graham put the seal on a memorable afternoon for the Reds with a third goal 16 minutes from time, but it was the own goal, a header Dixie Dean would have been proud of, that lingers in the memory and no Evertonian has ever been allowed to forget it.

EUROPEAN ADVENTURES

LIVERPOOL
FOOTBALL CLUB

99. A FLYING START

A new chapter in the club's history is about to begin as the Liverpool squad board a plane bound for Iceland ahead of their historic first game in continental competition.

The English champions are off to play the part-timers from KR Reykjavik in the preliminary round of the European Cup and for the 22-man travelling party it is a step into the unknown.

Manager Bill Shankly leads his players, coaching staff and directors up the steps for what would be a circuitous voyage to the Icelandic capital.

With no direct flights they first flew to London before catching another flight to Glasgow and then from there to Reykjavik, flying over a volcanic eruption in the sea along the way.

The match took place late the following afternoon at Iceland's national stadium, and although the Arctic sun was shining at kick-off, the temperature dipped considerably as the evening approached.

After just three minutes, young Scot, Gordon Wallace, scored to get Liverpool's European adventure off to the perfect start.

At the opposite end Tommy Lawrence was a virtual spectator but it wasn't until the second half that the Reds began to rack up the goals their superiority deserved.

A minute after the restart, Roger Hunt doubled the advantage and Wallace then notched another, while Phil Chisnall scored his first for the club before Hunt completed a satisfactory 5-0 rout.

A local newspaper suggested afterwards that Liverpool could have tripled their tally but five was more than enough to deem the second leg a formality.

It had been a gentle introduction to competitive European football but much sterner tests lay ahead.

G-ARWD
B·O·A·C

100. LA DOLCE VITA

Roger Hunt smashes home a right-footed thunderbolt to sensationally open the scoring in the 1965 European Cup semi-final against holders and reigning world champions Internazionale.

Only four minutes had elapsed when Ian Callaghan crossed from the right and Hunt swivelled to hit this unstoppable half-volley past a 'keeper who was left rooted to his line.

It was a goal that threatened to blow the roof off the Kop, and it stunned the star-studded visitors who could have been excused for not knowing what had just hit them.

With the red half of Merseyside already in an unparalleled state of euphoria following the club's Wembley heroics four days earlier, lengthy queues had been snaking around Anfield since midday and the exuberant home support frightened the life out of the Italians.

The tone for an amazing evening was set when injured stars Gerry Byrne and Gordon Milne were sent out to parade the recently-won FA Cup. If the noise was loud then, Hunt's strike raised the decibel level even higher.

Not even Sandro Mazzola's equaliser six minutes later – an away goal that would ultimately prove crucial in the tie – could quash the enthusiasm of the capacity crowd.

A well-worked free-kick routine, finished by Callaghan, restored Liverpool's lead before the break. Ian St John increased the margin of victory with a goal late in the second half.

The visitors had been well and truly beaten, and to the tune of 'Santa Lucia' the Kop famously informed them to 'Go Back To Italy'.

Anfield's first great European night still ranks as one of the best ever. Unfortunately, there was a second leg to come.

OL
CLUB

101. THE CALM BEFORE THE STORM

On the shoreline of the picturesque Lake Como, Ian St John and Ron Yeats take time to enjoy the stunning scenery while contemplating what awaits in the seething cauldron of the San Siro.

The European Cup semi-final second leg against Internazionale looms and with a 3-1 lead from the game at Anfield, Liverpool have one foot in the final.

For a club that was scraping about in the mid-to-lower reaches of Division Two when the continent's most prestigious club competition was first launched, it's some achievement.

Having now swept the honours board at home, Shankly's dream was for Liverpool to become the first British side to be crowned Kings of Europe.

St John and Yeats had been integral to all this success, but the challenge that lay ahead was their biggest yet.

Getting accustomed to the vagaries and contrasting cultures of European football had been a huge learning curve for everyone at the club and in Milan they would be dealt the harshest of lessons.

If taking on a world-class Inter team, hell-bent on revenge, was not hard enough, they also had to face the might of 90,000 baying Italian supporters in the most hostile of arenas.

Throw into that mix a sleepless night when the nearby church bells rang relentlessly plus an inept refereeing display that has been shrouded in controversy ever since and it all combines to explain just how difficult it was for Liverpool to prevail that night.

Two dubiously-allowed goals cancelled out the first leg advantage as early as the ninth minute, and from that position the cunning hosts went on to complete the comeback.

The Reds' maiden campaign in Europe had been brought to a bitter end but they would come back stronger and wiser for this eye-opening experience in northern Italy.

102. ALL BAR ONE

On a wet and miserable evening in Glasgow, Roger Hunt tries in vain to salvage Liverpool's dream of landing their first-ever European trophy.

What should have been a memorable occasion against Borussia Dortmund at Hampden Park, the 1966 European Cup Winners' Cup final turned out to be a huge anti-climax for the Reds.

The moment captured here, as Dortmund goalkeeper Hans Tilkowski denies Hunt by tipping the ball over, sums up a night that left 20,000 travelling Kopites distraught.

Although they greatly outnumbered their German counterparts, Liverpool's defeat of Celtic in the last four meant the bulk of neutral support went the way of their opponents.

The adverse weather conditions, coupled with live TV coverage, also meant the famous stadium was way short of its 130,000 capacity and the wide-open spaces on the terracing told a tale as grim as the end result.

The recently-crowned English champions failed to turn their greater possession into goals and were rocked when Siggi Held put Dortmund ahead early in the second half. Hunt equalised seven minutes later but in extra-time Dortmund snatched a farcical winner.

With Tommy Lawrence stranded on the edge of the box, Reinhard Libuda launched a speculative lob towards goal from 40 yards out. Ron Yeats rushed back in a desperate attempt to clear but the ball hit the post and unfortunately deflected off him into the net.

Liverpool's cup hopes had been cruelly dashed and although Hunt was to get his revenge over the Germans in the World Cup final two months later, success in Europe for the Reds would have to wait a bit longer.

103. RISING STAR CRUYFF STUNS THE KOP

The mist rolls in from the Mersey on a damp December night as Johan Cruyff sends Liverpool crashing out of the 1966/67 European Cup.

Sporting unfamiliar canary-yellow shirts, Ron Yeats, Tommy Smith and Chris Lawler are helpless to prevent the precocious youngster from inspiring Ajax to an aggregate victory.

Despite suffering an emphatic 5-1 first-leg defeat in Amsterdam the previous week, a typically rousing pre-match call-to-arms by Bill Shankly had instilled belief among Kopites.

Nearly 54,000 crammed into Anfield, steam rose from the Kop and overcrowding forced supporters to spill onto the side of the pitch.

Two Cruyff goals later, though, and those hopeful home fans had been stunned into submission. Although Roger Hunt also netted twice, a 2-2 draw was nowhere near enough and the under-rated Dutch champions deservedly took their place in the next round.

It was the start of a rise to greatness that would culminate in three successive European Cup wins in the early Seventies, with Cruyff featuring in all of them.

Liverpool would not grace the competition for another eight years, come which time Yeats had left the club. By the time Europe was eventually conquered in 1977 so too had Lawler, but for an ageing Smith there would be a fairy-tale end to his career and it was to come in this competition.

As for the unusual kit combination of yellow shirts and black shorts, it was only ever worn one other time – away to Arsenal in August 1967 but minus the badge on the shirt.

104. SNOW CHANCE

Add a bit of tinsel and you'd have a scene that wouldn't look out of place on a Christmas card but there is no festive cheer attached to this photograph – it is Roger Hunt kicking up a snowstorm on the night Liverpool slid out of the Inter Cities Fairs Cup in 1967/68.

Played on a blanket of ice just nine days into the new year, the conditions at Anfield were far better suited to the opposition, the famous Hungarian club Ferencvaros.

Holding a 1-0 advantage from the first meeting in Budapest, Ferencvaros, even without their star man Florian Albert, looked a class act from the first whistle.

On a treacherous surface their finely-tuned precision passing caused unease in the Liverpool ranks, and with the blond-haired Zoltan Varga pulling the strings it was no surprise when they took the lead.

What proved to be the only goal of the night came from Laszlo Branikovits on 19 minutes.

It was always going to be a tall order for the Reds to turn it around after that and although they had some chances, like the one pictured here, the visiting 'keeper Bela Takacs was in fine form.

Ferencvaros became the first team to inflict a home defeat on Liverpool in Europe and no-one could deny that they deserved it.

Having won the trophy in 1965, they went all the way to the final again this season but lost to Leeds United.

You can't beat'em

OCEAN
JOC INTERIOR

SERIAL WINNERS...1971-79

105. THE MIGHTY EMLYN

Emlyn Hughes consoles a crestfallen Alan Ball as they leave the pitch at the end of a thrilling all-Merseyside FA Cup semi-final in 1971.

The emotions at Old Trafford could not have been more contrasting. Ball's aspirations of cup glory have just been shattered, while Hughes is Wembley bound with Liverpool for the first time.

Liverpudlians celebrate a famous victory and the Everton captain is left to reflect on what might have been because until just before the hour mark, he had seemed destined to be the match-winner.

Reigning champions Everton went into the tie as slight favourites, and it was through Ball that they drew first blood after only 10 minutes.

In what was a pulsating encounter, the Reds continued to press and eventually got their reward in the 59th minute. Striker Alun Evans, the club's first £100,000 teenager, was the scorer, holding his nerve in front of the red hordes at the Stretford End with only the 'keeper to beat.

It was the turning point of the afternoon and with 18 minutes remaining, Brian Hall picked the perfect moment to score his first goal for the club, hammering home a half-volley that proved to be the decisive strike.

Epitomised by the spirit of Hughes, signed from Blackpool in February 1967 and still two years away from being captain, it was a comeback that showed the increasing maturity of this young Liverpool team, and although Arsenal would once again break Liverpudlian hearts in the final, Bill Shankly's second great side was coming of age.

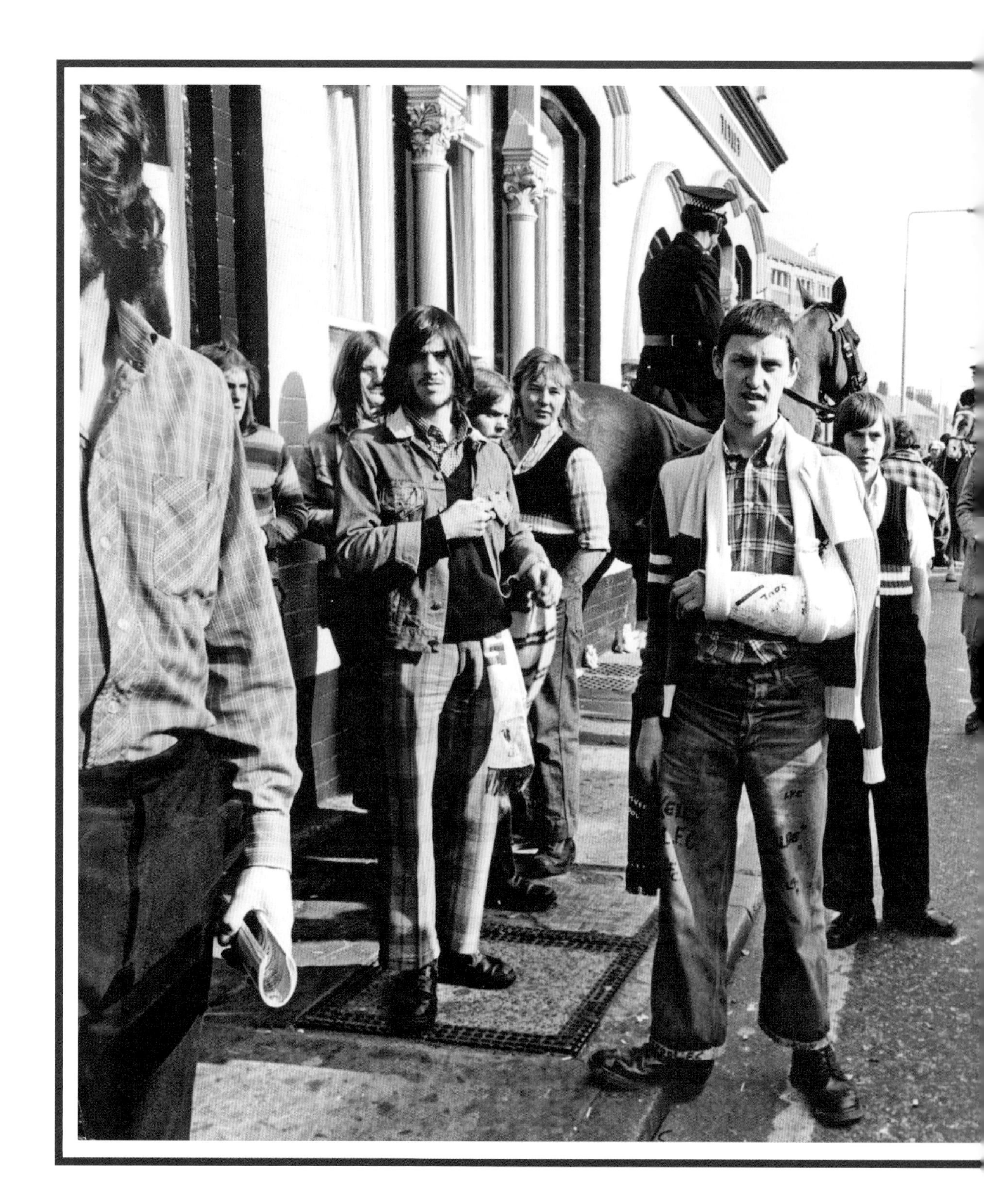

106. SATURDAY'S KIDS

A typical matchday scene outside the Albert pub on Walton Breck Road in early October 1972 as young supporters gather ahead of the Merseyside derby.

It's the era of glam rock and the likes of T-Rex, Slade and David Bowie are providing the soundtrack to the emergence of Shankly's young title pretenders.

In the fashion stakes, denim jackets, bell bottom trousers and tank tops are all the rage, AirWear boots are the popular choice of footwear, while scarves, silk or knitted, are tied more around the wrist than the neck.

It's even acceptable to wear opposition colours, as in the case of the lad on the left who is sporting a Leeds United scarf, possibly the spoils of victory acquired from the previous week's away trip.

Although mounted police are on the streets to control the growing crowds as kick-off approaches, in this group there is clear evidence of Reds and Blues mixing freely, with one lone supporter boldly displaying an Everton tattoo on his left arm.

As for the actual game they were about to go and see, it was to be an afternoon to remember for midfielder Peter Cormack, signed from Nottingham Forest just three months earlier.

In front of almost 56,000 on his derby debut, the Scotland international headed home the only goal 13 minutes from time, a result that extended Liverpool's lead at the top of the table.

107. SHANKLY IS OUR KING

Bill Shankly's rebuilding job is complete. His second great Liverpool team has come to fruition and a record-breaking eighth league championship has just been confirmed.

With a red silk scarf tied tightly around his neck and fists clenched in victorious defiance, Shankly stands proudly in front of a joyous Kop.

It's a title triumph that has been seven years in the making and the adulation for the manager is plain to see. In the words of ITV commentator Gerald Sindstat, "This is the man they love", and the respect was mutual.

The communion between the manager and the supporters had never been more profound than in this moment.

These emotional scenes of celebration came following a goalless draw at home to Leicester City on 28 April 1973. It brought Liverpool the point required to deliver what Shanks famously described as his 'bread and butter'.

Success in the league was what he strived for above everything else and after the near-miss of the previous season, plus the six trophy-less years before that, this was an occasion to savour.

Further redemption was to follow just a few weeks later in the form of Liverpool's first European trophy, yet within a year the great man had managed the Reds for the final time.

He bowed out having guided the club to three league titles, two FA Cups and the UEFA Cup, but left behind a far greater legacy, as the man who had built Liverpool up into a renowned 'bastion of invincibility'.

L.F.C.
L.F.C.

108. LITTLE BAMBER DOES IT AGAIN

For the second time in four seasons Brian Hall is a hero in the FA Cup semi-final and the advert on top of the stand is an ominous one for Liverpool's opponents: 'You Can't Beat'em'.

Nicknamed 'Little Bamber' due to his diminutive frame and academic background – Bamber being a reference to *University Challenge* host Bamber Gascoigne – the look on Hall's face suggests he can hardly believe it, but he's just opened the scoring in the 1974 replay against Leicester City at Villa Park.

Four days after a goalless draw at Old Trafford and a non-scoring first half here, the deadlock in the tie was eventually broken just a minute after the break.

Steve Heighway crossed from the left, John Toshack nodded it down and Keith Weller's intended clearance was deflected into the Holte End net off the head of Hall.

Kevin Keegan rushes to congratulate him while Peter Cormack and Alec Lindsay celebrate in the background.

Leicester hit back with an equaliser from Len Glover just two minutes later but Peter Shilton, in his stand-out all-white goalkeeper strip, was beaten twice more – by Keegan in the 66th minute and Toshack two minutes from time – as Liverpool booked a Wembley date with Newcastle United.

Although Hall's last-four winner against Everton in 1971 is more memorable and the most important of the 21 goals he registered for the Reds, this was undoubtedly a crucial one too, with the added bonus that on this occasion it ultimately paved the way to FA Cup glory come the end of the season.

beat'em
Dormie
HOME and AWAY
Drum

109. GOSH IT'S TOSH

Seventy thousand Catalans fall silent as John Toshack raises one arm in celebration after putting Liverpool on course for a historic victory at the Camp Nou.

It's the first leg of the 1976 UEFA Cup semi-final and no English team has ever previously beaten Barcelona here.

Only 13 minutes have elapsed and Toshack has given the Reds, kitted out on this night in Real Madrid-esque all-white, a crucial 1-0 lead.

A club record £110,000 signing from Cardiff in 1970, the popular Welshman was enjoying the most productive spell of his Liverpool career.

Normally the perfect foil for strike partner Kevin Keegan, on this occasion the roles were reversed. Cleverly evading his marker, Tosh was played through on goal by Keegan

and, from 12 yards out, made no mistake with a firmly-struck right-footed finish.

With an early lead against a star-studded Barca team that included the celebrated Dutch Johans, Cruyff and Neeskens, Bob Paisley's Liverpool then proceeded to produce one of the club's finest European away performances.

They reduced the aforementioned duo to bit-part roles and held on comfortably. Had they scored another four or five there could have been no complaints, such was their superiority on the night.

The home fans were so incensed with their side's performance that the white handkerchiefs came out long before the final whistle and a barrage of cushions rained down on the pitch as Liverpool celebrated a famous victory, the importance of which was not fully realised until after the second leg a fortnight later.

In becoming the first English team to win at the Camp Nou, Liverpool took a major step towards securing their place in a second UEFA Cup final, and a 1-1 draw at Anfield completed the job.

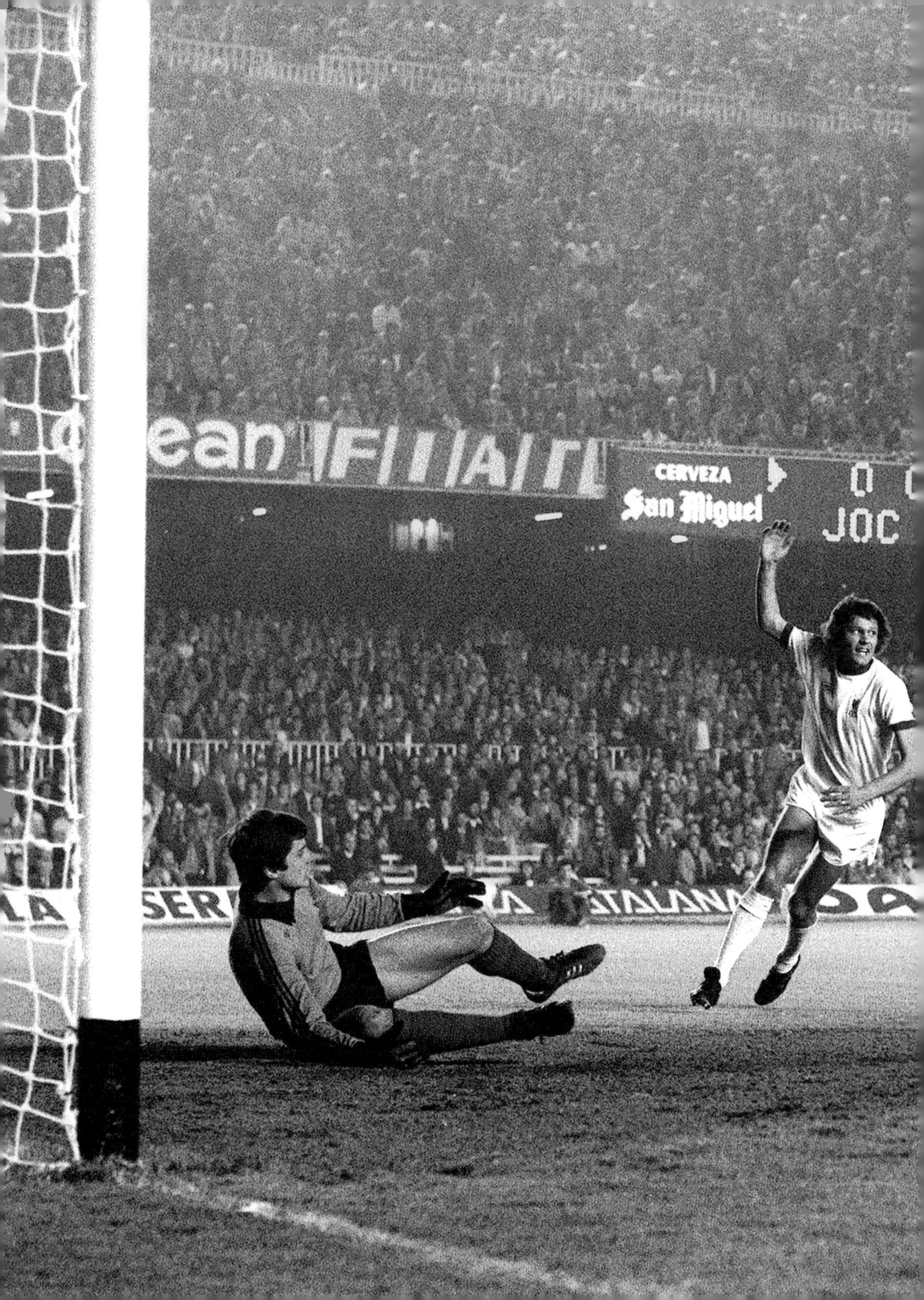
CERVEZA
San Miguel
0 0
JOC

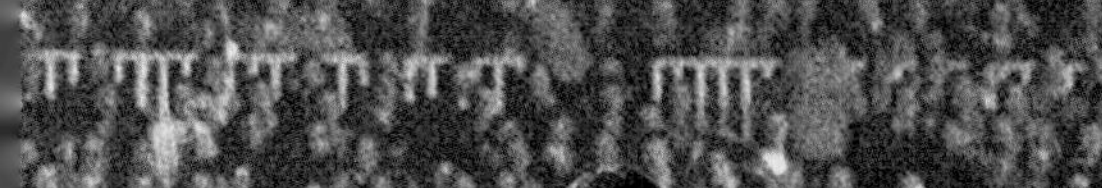

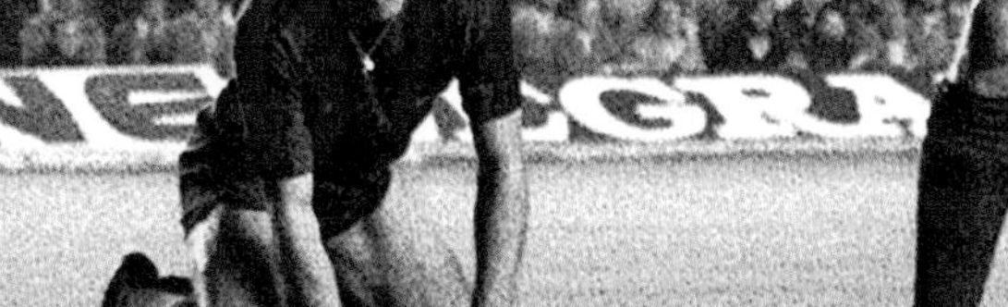

CERVEZA
San Miguel

110. THE GREAT FIRST DIVISION DRAMA

With a beaming smile and his arms aloft in jubilation, Footballer of the Year, Kevin Keegan, has just broken the brave resistance of Wolverhampton Wanderers and put the destiny of the 1975/76 league title firmly back in Liverpool hands.

On a night of unbearable tension at Molineux, Wolves goalkeeper Gary Pierce lies grounded after Keegan's equaliser, a close-range finish in the 74th minute, sparks a mass outpouring of joy and relief among the travelling throng of Kopites.

The front cover of the matchday programme had billed this game as 'The Great First Division Drama' and it didn't disappoint.

In what was the final league game of the season, the Reds journeyed to the Black Country on 4 May, knowing a win or a low scoring draw would be enough to see them overtake leaders Queens Park Rangers and clinch an unprecedented ninth league title.

The task facing the home side was equally complicated and they had to take maximum points just to be in with a chance of avoiding relegation.

Over 20,000 Liverpudlians swamped Wolverhampton, but there was a shock in store when Steve Kindon fired the hosts into an early lead.

The score remained that way until deep into the second half when Keegan eased Liverpool's nerves with his goal and then the floodgates opened as further strikes from John Toshack (also pictured here) and Ray Kennedy – in the final five minutes – put the outcome beyond any doubt.

It had been one of the most thrilling nights in Liverpool's history, Bob Paisley had clinched his first trophy as manager and the parties continued on the M6 all the way home.

800

111. SUPER CALLY

The club's all-time record appearance holder, Ian Callaghan, is pictured at Anfield in 1977 commemorating his landmark 800th game for the Reds – a feat not matched by any other Liverpool player before or since.

In a highly distinguished career that spanned almost two decades, Toxteth-born Callaghan, who had made his first-team debut as a fresh-faced teenager back in April 1960, was a shining example of everything that is good about the game.

A true gentleman in every sense of the word, the winger-turned-midfielder would be the only player to survive Liverpool's fairy-tale journey from life as a mediocre Second Division outfit to the lofty summit of European football. Along the way he won almost every honour possible, including the highest respect from his fellow professionals and the adulation of the fans.

The ever-popular Cally was also voted Footballer of the Year in 1974 and booked only once in 18 years.

His milestone 800th appearance was originally believed to have come in a 3-1 home win against Derby County in February 1977, an occasion on which the players formed a guard of honour for him as he emerged from the tunnel.

Only in later years, when Charity Shield games started to be recognised as competitive fixtures were the stats amended meaning official records now show that his 800th game was actually an FA Cup replay away to Crystal Palace a month earlier.

Either way, when this photograph was taken Callaghan was soon to turn 35, yet still found the opportunity to chalk up even more appearances, taking his official tally to 857 before time was eventually called on his lengthy and illustrious Liverpool career the following year.

It's a record that is unlikely to ever be beaten.

112. SUPERSUB STRIKES AGAIN

Anfield is about to be shaken to its core and David Fairclough is set to experience a life-changing moment as one of the most iconic moments in Liverpool history unfolds in front of a heaving Spion Kop.

It's the European Cup quarter-final second leg, Liverpool lead 2-1 on the night but it's 2-2 on aggregate and St Etienne are heading through on the away goals rule.

Following a 1-0 defeat in France, Kevin Keegan had put the Reds back on level terms after just two minutes, but Dominique Bathenay restored the visitors' advantage with a stunning long-range strike early in the second half.

Ray Kennedy provided a glimmer of hope as the Reds regained the lead on the night and over 55,000 remained transfixed by a tie that hung intriguingly in the balance.

But with the clock ticking, Liverpool's hopes of lifting a first European Cup were dwindling fast.

In the 74th minute Bob Paisley unleashed his secret weapon, a young flame-haired Scouse striker who had developed a knack of coming off the bench to score vital goals.

Ten minutes later Kennedy played a hopeful ball over the top and, wrestling free from the shackles of the St Etienne defenders, Fairclough latched onto it. As he closed in on goal, time seemed to stand still and everyone in the ground held their breath.

For someone who had only just turned 20, Liverpool's number 12 remained remarkably composed and proceeded to coolly side-foot the ball under the body of goalkeeper Ivan Curkovic.

Seconds later Anfield erupted, and the Reds advanced another step towards the final in Rome.

For many it was a night that will forever rank as the best and the legend of Supersub has echoed ever since.

113. KINGS OF EUROPE

European supremacy has finally been accomplished and the players proudly parade the continent's most glittering prize around the Stadio Olimpico in Rome.

It follows a never-to-be-forgotten 3-1 victory over Borussia Moenchengladbach, which confirmed Liverpool Football Club as the undisputed champions of Europe for the first time.

Captain Emlyn Hughes and midfielder Jimmy Case each have a firm grip on the trophy while Steve Heighway, Ray Kennedy, Tommy Smith and Phil Neal are also at the forefront of the celebrations.

With a near 30,000-strong legion of Liverpudlians joining them on a pilgrimage to the Eternal City, a sea of red and white chequered flags formed an impressive backdrop to the triumph.

Just days after suffering the heartache of defeat in the FA Cup final, Bob Paisley's Reds, lifted by such wonderful support, produced a near-perfect performance to overpower the champions of West Germany.

They took a first-half lead through a sweetly-struck Terry McDermott shot, but a rare lapse in concentration allowed Allan Simonsen to equalise shortly after the break.

In true 'Roy of the Rovers' style Smith, a veteran of the club's first European campaign and just days ahead of his testimonial, then powered home a header to restore the advantage.

A truly historic success was secured eight minutes from time after Kevin Keegan, playing his last-ever competitive game in a red shirt, was brought down in the box by Borussia captain Berti Vogts.

Neal stepped up to take the penalty and calmly sent Wolfgang Kneib the wrong way to seal the crowning glory of Liverpool's remarkable rise to the top.

From Reykjavik to Rome, it was the conclusion of a 13-year odyssey, but also the start of a glorious reign for the new Kings of Europe.

114. HIT FOR SIX

Jimmy Case welcomes a familiar face back to Anfield as the players emerge from the tunnel for the second leg of the European Super Cup final in December 1977.

Just six months after leaving the Reds to join SV Hamburg, Kevin Keegan returned to his former home ground in the colours of his new club.

His much-hyped comeback added extra intrigue to this annual contest between the holders of the European Cup and European Cup Winners' Cup, played back then over two legs on a home and away basis.

The first meeting in West Germany had finished 1-1, but it would be a completely different story on Merseyside.

While a lot of the pre-match build-up focused on the inevitable comparisons between Keegan and his replacement in the Liverpool number seven shirt, Kenny Dalglish, it was Terry McDermott who stole the show, grabbing his first-ever hat-trick in an emphatic 6-0 rout.

Keegan, who had received a warm welcome from the Kop, groaned: "Liverpool look as strong, if not stronger, as they ever were. I didn't think Liverpool would play as well as that. We are not as bad a team as we looked but Liverpool scored six and could have had more."

The reigning English and European champions had created yet more history, becoming the first English winners of the Super Cup, while the margin of victory matched the previous best between Ajax v AC Milan in 1972.

As for Case, there would soon be another honour heading his way as the inaugural recipient of the Bravo Award, given to the most outstanding young footballer in Europe that year.

umbro
LFC
HSV
HSV

115. THE BOSS OF BOSSES

The most successful English football manager of all time stalks the Anfield touchline during a league game at home to Leicester City in April 1978.

A humble genius who reluctantly stepped up to replace Bill Shankly in 1974, Bob Paisley oversaw the accumulation of a record-breaking 14 major trophies during his nine years in charge of Liverpool.

The club had never enjoyed a more dominant period of prolonged success and, when this picture was taken, they were just a month away from becoming the first British side to retain the European Cup. Not that you could tell by the look on Paisley's face here.

Just five minutes into this match he was faced with a major problem and was forced to come down early from his usual seat in the directors' box.

David Johnson, sitting in the dugout that former bricklayer Paisley had actually built back in the 1950s, had just limped out of the action with a serious knee injury that would ultimately rule him out for the remainder of the season.

To Paisley's right, coach Ronnie Moran gives some last-minute instructions to young substitute Sammy Lee, who went on to mark his debut with a goal in a 3-2 victory.

This was the fifth fixture of an unbeaten home run that would eventually stretch to a club record 85 games, spanning almost three years.

Ironically, it was Leicester City who eventually ended the sequence in January 1981, but thankfully that was nothing more than a minor setback.

Four months later Bob Paisley guided Liverpool to a third European Cup in Paris.

116. SEVENTH HEAVEN

With his distinctive 'Scouse' perm, Terry McDermott wheels away in delight after scoring his most famous goal and supporters in the Main Stand rise to their feet in appreciation.

Tottenham Hotspur, with their Argentine World Cup stars Osvaldo Ardiles and Ricky Villa, have just been taught a footballing lesson and sent packing on the wrong end of a 7-0 annihilation in September 1978.

It's a game that will forever be eulogised about and one that left even the most seasoned of observers struggling to find new superlatives to explain what they had witnessed.

Bob Paisley's reigning European champions were in imperious form as they laid down an ominous marker to those who threatened to challenge them for the title.

Two Kenny Dalglish goals inside the first 20 minutes set the tone and by the interval Ray Kennedy had added another. A David Johnson double made it 5-0 before Phil Neal's twice-taken penalty brought a sixth.

It's the final goal that's imprinted on the memory though. It came 14 minutes from time and started from a rare Tottenham corner at the Kop end, which Liverpool quickly cleared.

Dalglish supplied Johnson, out on the right, and his raking cross-field pass picked out Steve Heighway who was racing down the opposite flank.

From Heighway's perfectly-weighted centre, an in-rushing McDermott applied the finishing touch, heading the ball in at the far post.

The Kirkby-born midfielder was no stranger to scoring spectacular goals but even by his high standards this was something special.

It was a fluent attacking move from one end of the pitch to the other that ripped the opposition apart in just a matter of seconds.

Paisley described it as the best he had ever seen, and few would argue. It was the perfect finish to the perfect performance.

THE KING

117. WHEN KENNY MET CALLY

Three years before they became team-mates, Celtic's Kenny Dalglish tussles with Ian Callaghan while Phil Thompson looks on during a game at Parkhead in August 1974.

The Reds were in Glasgow to play a testimonial for legendary Celtic skipper Billy McNeill and it was to be the only time Dalglish ever lined up against Liverpool.

He was 23 at the time but already an established star north of the border, having represented Scotland in that summer's World Cup in West Germany.

It could have all been different though had Liverpool not allowed him to slip through their scouting net eight years earlier.

As a 15-year-old in 1966, Dalglish was invited to Melwood for a week-long trial and actually pulled on the red shirt in a 'B' team game against Southport.

When Liverpool failed to follow up their initial interest, he was snapped up by Celtic. After progressing through the ranks, his form was starting to turn heads in England and it seemed only a matter of time before he would be seeking a new challenge.

The start of the new season was just days away when this meeting took place and the game ended 1-1.

Although Dalglish was substituted at the interval, new Liverpool boss Bob Paisley made a note of what he had seen and would keep a close eye on the situation over the next few years.

118. A WARM WELCOME FOR THE GOLDEN 'BHOY'

The new heir to the Kop throne, Kenneth Mathieson Dalglish, poses for the camera with three young Kopites on his first day as a Liverpool player in August 1977.

The ink had not yet dried on the contract but already Dalglish was being made to feel welcome at his new home.

The Reds had just broken the British transfer record to acquire his services and it gave the team a massive boost going into the 1977/78 season. Although they had won the European Cup just three months earlier, Kevin Keegan had gone, and his boots were big ones to fill.

Bob Paisley had reportedly been monitoring other players as potential replacements, notably Birmingham's Trevor Francis and Arsenal's Liam Brady, but the Scot was always his number one choice.

Dalglish was the only candidate truly capable of inheriting Keegan's iconic number seven shirt and meeting the huge expectations that came with it.

Preparations for the new campaign were well underway when he arrived and three days later the 26-year-old would make his debut at Wembley in the Charity Shield against Manchester United.

At Anfield, as we see here, work was ongoing to get the ground ready for his first home game, with new fences and barriers, some yet to be painted, having been installed on the Kop.

After scoring on the opening day of the season, away to Middlesbrough, Dalglish then marked his first two appearances in L4 with goals against Newcastle and West Brom.

The new boy had hit the ground running and would only get better. Come the end of the season it was his goal that clinched Liverpool's second European Cup and that record transfer fee was already proving to be a sound investment.

adidas
LIVERPOOL FC
adidas

119. CLOSE ENCOUNTERS IN THE THIRD STRIP

In Liverpool's rarely-worn first all-yellow kit, Kenny Dalglish's silky skills attract the unwanted close attention of Southampton pair Malcolm Waldron and Steve Williams at The Dell in September 1979.

The previous season's Footballer of the Year, Dalglish had settled seamlessly into the Liverpool team and just two years into his career south of the border was already one of the most feared forwards in the First Division.

He topped the club goalscoring charts in his first two seasons, netting 31 and 25 times respectively, but there was much more to his game than goals.

A selfless team player who brought others into play, he was an on-pitch visionary who could spot an opening that the naked eye of most would never see.

A world-class football brain perfectly complemented his superb ball control, and although never the fastest in terms of pace, Dalglish's speed of thought always kept him one step ahead of his rivals.

He helped take Liverpool to another level and 1979/80 would see them continue to exert their domestic dominance by successfully defending the title they had won a year before.

On this late summer afternoon down on the south coast, however, the champions suffered a rare off-day and not even the magic of Dalglish could prevent a 3-2 defeat against the Saints.

Trevor Hebberd, Phil Boyer and Charlie George netted for the hosts, with David Johnson and Colin Irwin replying for Liverpool.

ALL YOU NEED IS RUSH

120. POACHER

An ominous warning was issued to opposition defenders across the land on 10 October 1981 when the greatest goalscorer Liverpool Football Club has ever known opened his league account for the Reds.

Pictured here is the second of two goals a teenage Ian Rush scored against Leeds United on this day and it confirmed his arrival on the big stage.

In the white shirts, Paul Hart, Trevor Cherry and Frank Gray are left stranded as Rush slides the ball in at the Kop end, while watching on is Kenny Dalglish, the master overseeing the work of his young apprentice.

Signed from Chester City the previous year, the rookie striker had already netted against Oulu Palloseura in the European Cup and Exeter City in the League Cup.

But in what was his eighth league outing for the Reds, and his first of this campaign, he served notice of his vast potential and immediately dispelled any doubts over his ability to make the grade.

It took him just 18 minutes to register the first goal, shooting through a crowd of legs from the edge of the box after turning sharply when receiving a pass from Graeme Souness.

In what turned out to be a routine victory against the team propping up the rest of the First Division, Leeds captain Cherry then doubled Liverpool's advantage when putting the ball into his own goal midway through the half.

Rush worked tirelessly throughout and was rewarded for his dogged persistence up front a minute from time when he scored this goal from close range to wrap up a 3-0 victory.

Within the space of just 11 days, he had netted his first five senior goals and there were plenty more to come. Another 341 to be precise, putting him way out in front as the club's all-time record goalscorer.

HAFNIA
W.J.H
INSURANCE
SANATA
publicom

RFW

121. TORMENTOR

Nothing screams the early to mid-1980s more than an Adidas Tango football, Liverpool's pin-striped red kit and an Ian Rush goal against Everton – all of which are captured here in the Merseyside derby at Goodison Park on 6 November 1982.

It was an occasion no Liverpudlian will ever tire of discussing, the day Rush wrote his name indelibly into local folklore with four goals in an amazing 5-0 win.

Despite his boyhood preference for the blue side of the city, the Welsh striker quickly became their chief tormentor, and it was his performance on this unforgettable afternoon that really laid down the marker for what was to come.

He set the ball rolling after just 11 minutes and doubled the advantage early in the second half. Mark Lawrenson added a third before Liverpool's number nine regained centre stage to complete his hat-trick, the first in this fixture since 1935.

Just when the home supporters thought it could get no worse came the moment that is pictured.

It shows Rush, having latched onto a Sammy Lee through ball and rounded goalkeeper Neville Southall, coolly side-footing into an empty net at the Park End.

David Hodgson can be seen in the background while Blues full-back Brian Borrows makes a forlorn attempt to get back.

On the Gwladys Street terrace, where Rush had once stood, Evertonians could only look on in disbelief. Their team had been ripped apart almost single-handedly by a striker who would continue to give them nightmares.

No player has scored more goals (25) in the Merseyside derby and Liverpudlians still gleefully sing about the four he scored on this day.

HIGSONS
HAFNIA
DANISH MEATS
INSURANCE

122. PREDATOR

Another ball nestles sweetly into the back of the opposition net as Liverpool's master marksman darts off to celebrate in the rain-soaked Romanian capital of Bucharest.

It's April 1984 and the second leg of the European Cup semi-final, a tie that began on a knife-edge until Ian Rush produced the goods once again.

With just a slender 1-0 lead from the first leg, Joe Fagan's Reds faced a tough task, not helped by the intimidating atmosphere that greeted them.

The intense hostility was a result of an incident at Anfield involving captain Graeme Souness that left a Dinamo Bucharest player with a broken jaw.

Targeted at every opportunity, Souness revelled in the vitriol that came his way though, and it was he who supplied the killer pass from which this goal was scored.

The finish was Rush at his predatory best – one touch to get the ball under control, another to bypass the defender, and then a delicate dink over the outrushing goalkeeper.

Only 11 minutes had gone, and Liverpool had a vital away goal that took the sting out of what threatened to be a volatile contest.

As the home crowd sit in silence under umbrellas, Ronnie Whelan chases after Rush and the Reds are on their way to Rome for the final.

Costel Orac equalised for the hosts late in the first half and although the outcome was never in real doubt, Liverpool's most lethal weapon made certain with a second six minutes from time.

In terms of goals scored, the 1983/84 season was to be Rush's finest and he netted 47 times, a club record and enough to win him the European Golden Boot.

E PRIN SPO
tex
ROMANIA
'84·OCTOBER 11-21

crown paints
OLYMPIASTADION MUEHCHEN
FC BAYERN -
FC LIVERPOOL
0 : 1
22. APRIL 1981
LIVERPOOL
ROME 77
WEMBLEY 78
EUROPES No1

EXTRAORDINARY ERA...1980s

On a famous night in Munich's Olympic Stadium, Liverpool supporters celebrate a crucial Ray Kennedy goal in the second leg of the 1981 European Cup semi-final.

As the scoreboard shows, Kennedy's 83rd-minute strike had just given Bob Paisley's team a 1-0 lead over Bayern and with the first meeting at Anfield having finished goalless, a place in the final was all but secured.

So confident had the West German champions been of emerging victorious on home soil that leaflets were handed out to their fans on the way into the ground, outlining directions to Paris for the final.

Captain Paul Breitner had also vociferously dismissed Liverpool's chances ahead of the game, but in doing so he wrote the Reds manager's pre-match team-talk for him.

Inspired by the over-confidence of the Germans they were fired up like never before, and not even a crippling injury list could divert their focus.

A makeshift defence including Colin Irwin and Richard Money repelled everything the hosts had to throw at them, while rookie winger Howard Gayle, an early replacement for the limping Kenny Dalglish, ran the Bayern defence ragged.

By the time he was himself substituted late in the second half, Liverpool were in the ascendancy and Kennedy's goal confirmed their superiority on the night.

Because of that all-important away goal, not even an equaliser from Karl-Heinz Rummenigge four minutes later could deny them their ticket to the final and a date with Real Madrid.

Paisley rated it as the club's finest away performance in Europe, and after a night of partying in Munich's famous Bierkellers, these celebrating Scousers were off making plans for a trip to 'Gay Paree'.

From back to front (Liverpool players only): *Alan Hansen, Ronnie Whelan, Ian Rush, Craig Johnston, Phil Neal, Sammy Lee, Kenny Dalglish, Bruce Grobbelaar, Graeme Souness.*

124. LOST IN LODZ

In a setting so far removed from the glitz and glamour of the modern-day Champions League, Graeme Souness leads Liverpool out for the first leg of the European Cup quarter-final away to Widzew Lodz in March 1983.

With that renowned look of determination etched across his face there was certainly no finer captain in situations like this than Souness. Unfortunately, for the man directly behind him, goalkeeper Bruce Grobbelaar, it would be a night to forget.

The Reds went into the tie as strong favourites but, as those who had witnessed the recent defeats in Tbilisi (1979) and Sofia (1982) would testify, these trips to Eastern Europe were never easy.

Yet despite the Arctic conditions in this industrial heartland of central Poland, the Reds were in control until Grobbelaar mishandled what should have been a routine catch four minutes into the second half.

Miroslaw Tlokinski capitalised to break the deadlock and the game turned. Ten minutes from the end, substitute Wieslaw Wraga scored a decisive second to spark celebratory bonfires on the terraces.

In front of a full house at Anfield a fortnight later, hopes remained high that Liverpool could, for the first time in their European history, overturn a 2-0 deficit, but it wasn't to be.

Although a 3-2 victory on the night salvaged some pride, Bob Paisley's dream of winning a fourth European Cup before stepping down as manager was over.

For Souness, Grobbelaar and the rest, another opportunity was just around the corner.

The look of sheer bliss on their faces says it all; Alan Kennedy's penalty has just hit the back of the net and Liverpool are champions of Europe for a fourth time.

Alan Hansen leads the sprint to congratulate the goalscoring hero, Michael Robinson leaps for joy, while Mark Lawrenson and Sammy Lee seem set for take-off. Behind them, Ronnie Whelan and Steve Nicol embrace, and the Curva Nord of Rome's Stadio Olimpico is ablaze with red and white.

With the odds stacked against them like never before, Joe Fagan's treble-chasing Reds of 1984 had been cast in the role of sacrificial lambs entering the lion's den of their opponents' home ground.

The travelling Liverpudlians were vastly outnumbered and so sure of victory were the hosts

that street carnivals had already been planned in readiness.

But with inspirational captain Graeme Souness leading from the front, the English champions boldly swaggered into the Italian capital singing the Chris Rea hit 'I Don't Know What It Is But I Love It' and quickly silenced the vociferous locals.

A Phil Neal goal drew first blood, only for Roberto Pruzzo to level just before the break. There was to be no further scoring in open play, and for the first time ever the European Cup final was to be decided on penalties.

Scouse hearts skipped a beat when Nicol blazed over but Bruce Grobbelaar's antics and clinical finishing by Neal, Souness, Ian Rush and Kennedy ensured the big trophy headed back to Anfield. The Eternal City had been conquered for a second time and it was a case of 'Campioni Liverpool!'

Left to right: *Alan Hansen, Michael Robinson, Mark Lawrenson, Ronnie Whelan, Steve Nicol (back to camera), Sammy Lee, Hans Harryson (linesman)*

126. BIG JAN KEEPS HIS COOL

On a tension-packed night at Vicarage Road, Jan Molby steps up to the penalty spot with the responsibility for keeping Liverpool in the FA Cup resting on his broad shoulders.

Just four minutes remain of this FA Cup quarter-final replay in March 1986 and, with Watford leading 1-0, fingernails had been chewed to the bone and nerves were shredded.

Following a frustrating goalless draw on Merseyside six nights earlier, future Liverpool star John Barnes had put The Hornets ahead with a superbly-struck free-kick just after the break.

As home fans anxiously checked their watches, Liverpool, resplendent in all-white, pushed forward frantically.

With their hopes fading fast they were finally rewarded for their relentless perseverance when Tony Coton brought down Ian Rush inside the box and the referee immediately pointed to the spot.

For all their domestic dominance over the previous decade, success in this competition had annoyingly eluded the Reds and the prospect of another elimination was not one that any of the 10,000 travelling supporters, or all those back home listening on the radio, wished to contemplate.

This burning desire for FA Cup glory was shared by the team, for whom there wasn't a winner's medal among them and, as Molby takes the kick, Steve McMahon can be seen in the background praying that he scored.

The Great Dane had only assumed spot-kick duties earlier that season but, with the pressure on, he kept his cool to slot the ball home from 12 yards. It was one of 42 penalties he would convert for the club and was arguably his most important.

Ian Rush later scored the winner in extra-time and the season ended with Liverpool lifting the FA Cup at Wembley for the first time in 12 years.

crown
paints

adidas
adidas

127. SUMMER VIBES

On their first day of pre-season training at Melwood, John Barnes and Peter Beardsley, the club's two big summer signings in 1987, receive a welcoming arm around the shoulder from manager Kenny Dalglish.

On the back of a trophy-less 1986/87 campaign, and with Ian Rush having left to join Juventus, the manager was rebuilding the team and an exciting new era beckoned for Liverpool.

Having already brought John Aldridge on board, the dual capture of Barnes and Beardsley completed an attacking triumvirate that would take the First Division by storm.

Barnes and Beardsley were no strangers to Liverpool supporters. Both had opposed the Reds on a number of occasions for their respective former clubs during the previous few years and Dalglish had long been a big admirer of the pair.

Team-mates at international level with England, having both been at the 1986 World Cup, their niche in the club history books was assured even before they pulled on the red shirt; Barnes as Liverpool's first high-profile black player and Beardsley as the then most expensive.

First to arrive was Jamaica-born Barnes, an electrifying left-winger, signed in mid-June from Watford for £900,000.

Beardsley, a skilful forward whose playing style drew comparisons with that of Dalglish, followed a month later and Liverpool had to break the British transfer record to get him, paying Newcastle £1.9 million.

Eyebrows were raised at the massive financial outlay on this sensational double swoop, but it proved to be an inspired decision and the money spent would soon be more than justified.

128. SUCCESS WITH A SAMBA BEAT

Despite Trevor Hebberd's best efforts, John Barnes whips in a cross from the left flank on his eagerly-anticipated Anfield debut against Oxford United in September 1987.

Recent signing Barnes had hit the ground running for the Reds but a collapsed sewer beneath the Kop meant Liverpool's first three games of the season were played away from home, delaying his official introduction to the home fans.

During this time, he raised the levels of expectation with his dynamic performances and queues had been snaking around the ground from mid-morning as supporters clamoured to see if the hype surrounding him was true.

They didn't have to wait long for an answer. Those lucky enough to gain admission gave the new number ten a tremendous reception and, in return, were treated to a masterclass.

With an awesome blend of poise, pace, strength and skill, Barnes was Brazilian-like in his play and whenever he gained possession an air of excitement would sweep through the stands.

He had supporters in the Kemlyn Road on the edge of their seats throughout the first half and soon had them on their feet too.

It was from this centre of his, pictured, that John Aldridge steered the ball into the net for the opening Anfield goal of the season after 13 minutes.

Then, eight minutes before the break, Barnes opened his Liverpool goalscoring account. It came via a free-kick just outside the box that Peter Beardsley played short to him before he curled the ball over the wall and beyond goalkeeper Peter Hucker.

That was the end of the scoring for this day, but Liverpudlians had themselves a new favourite, who would have plenty more tricks up his sleeve throughout the remainder of an unforgettable season.

129. ALDO STRIKES BACK

John Aldridge laps up the adulation of Liverpool fans at Selhurst Park after scoring the first goal of his hat-trick against Charlton Athletic on the opening day of the 1988/89 season.

It's the perfect response to those who suggested his place in the team was under threat following the recent return to Anfield of club legend Ian Rush.

Despite finishing the previous campaign as the First Division's top scorer, Aldridge was judged by many to be the most likely candidate to make way for Rush, but on the back of two goals in the Charity Shield a week earlier, this treble made it even more difficult for the manager to drop him.

The moustachioed marksman's similarities with Rush were not just confined to looks. He had a similar knack of hitting the back of the net and possessed an impressive goalscoring record.

Strong in the air and a selfless forward runner, the boyhood Kopite fulfilled a dream when joining the Reds from Oxford United and, as the reigning champions got their title defence off to a winning start here, it was clear that he wasn't going to give up his shirt without a fight.

In that iconic Candy-sponsored silver/grey strip, Aldridge opened the scoring after 23 minutes, stooping to head a John Barnes cross past former Reds reserve Bob Bolder in the Charlton goal.

Liverpool's number eight then went on to complete his hat-trick with a further two strikes in quick succession early in the second half.

Although he managed to retain his place throughout the season, often alongside Rush, sceptics said they couldn't play together, even if the stats

proved otherwise, and, just over a year after this photograph was taken, Aldridge was eventually deemed surplus to requirements and sold to Real Sociedad.

130. END OF AN ERA

As another triumphant campaign draws to a close, player-manager Kenny Dalglish and club captain Alan Hansen lead the champions on a familiar victory parade around Anfield.

The club's 18th league title had been secured the previous weekend and, following a 1-0 victory over Derby County, they would be presented with the spoils of their season-long endeavours.

For Dalglish and Hansen, this is now a photograph of added poignancy. Not only was it their last victorious celebration as Liverpool players, it's also the last time Liverpudlians would see them pictured on the pitch together.

Although Dalglish continued as manager for another year, he officially hung up his boots after bringing himself on for the last 19 minutes of this game; his first outing of the campaign doubling up as his 515th and final competitive appearance for the Reds.

A knee injury had ruled Hansen out of the fixture but in his official capacity as skipper, he still donned his kit to join the lap of honour and receive the trophy.

No-one knew at the time, but that championship-clinching match three days earlier was to be the last he ever played.

The injury was a persistent one and, after several failed comebacks in the reserves the following season, it eventually forced him to call time on what had been an illustrious career.

Hansen bowed out having made 620 appearances for the club and with a medal collection to rival the best. One of the greatest centre-backs in Liverpool history, he'd been such an important presence in the team since the late Seventies and replacing him proved to be a monumental task.

The club was about to enter a huge period of change and this title success in 1990 would grow in significance as the years passed.

ACKNOWLEDGEMENTS

In no particular order, the authors would like to thank the following, without whom the publication of this book would not have been possible...

Friends and family.

The staff at Reach Sport; notably Roy Gilfoyle, Colin Sumpter, Lee Ashun, Rick Cooke, Paul Dove and Steve Hanrahan.

Paul Hepworth, Stephen Done and Ian Wallace at Liverpool Football Club.

A special mention to Adrian Killen for all his help in terms of research and sourcing of photographs. Also, Jonny Stokkeland, Ged Rea, Eric Doig, Andy Marsden, Jeff Goulding, Kieran Smith, Kjell Hanssen, Jim Donnelly, Peter Raath, Arthur Ellinson, Rob Sawyer and Gareth Willsher.

Other invaluable research sources include The Official LFC Archives, LFChistory.net, Playupliverpool.com, The Unofficial Liverpool Football Club Museum, Liverpool FC Historical Group and The British Newspaper Archive.

Dave Cottrell and Will Hughes from the Official Liverpool FC Matchday Programme/Magazine.

And, last, but definitely not least, all the photographers who originally captured the moments that have been brought back to life on these pages.

Photographs sourced from Mirrorpix, Liverpool Football Club, Getty Images, Colorsport and private collections.

Share your thoughts about the book via our dedicated social media accounts:
Twitter – @OldLFC_Colour
Instagram – oldlfc_colour
Facebook – Old Liverpool FC In Colour